Advanced Praise for *The Champion Teammate*

"I highly recommend Jerry and John's new book *The Champion Teammate*. The book is a thought-provoking and insightful look into the dynamics of teamwork and how to build effective teams. Jerry and John draw on their extensive experience as mentor coaches and consultants to provide practical strategies for fostering trust, communication, and collaboration among team members. The book is well written and easy to read, making it accessible to both coaches and players. It is a valuable resource for anyone looking to improve their teamwork skills and create a more productive and engaged team. A must read for any professional mentor looking to build a winning team."

—*Cindy Timchal, coach, eight-time NCAA champion in women's lacrosse, US Lacrosse Hall of Fame*

"Jerry has done it again, this time teaming up with his friend and colleague John O'Sullivan to address perhaps one of the most important topics in sports today: how being an extraordinary teammate is the glue to the success and sustainability of every championship culture. Their new book, *The Champion Teammate*, is filled with inspirational and timeless lessons that we can use in elevating our team environment where all can be themselves, feel safe and connected, experience more joy, be competitive, and thrive. At Carolina, we place a high premium on coaching our athletes into being the best teammates possible. I can't wait to get copies of this brilliant book into the hands of our athletes and raise their levels of love, caring, leadership, and competitiveness."

—*Anson Dorrance, head coach, University North Carolina women's soccer, 22-time national champions, and 1991 USA World Cup champion coach*

"Here is a powerful work on the vital intersection of leadership, character, and culture—the team. Performance and winning matter, but victory feels short-lived and hollow if achieved without feeling love and connection throughout your team—every contributor from coach to the most junior member of the group. Moreover, great results are far less likely without a special sense of belonging and commitment, reverence for one's teammates and the team's mission, and the effort and courage that flows from these powerful feelings. *The Champion Teammate* unlocks a compelling set of concepts and behaviors that enable you, as a teammate, to create fertile ground for the character development of all involved, and to grow the culture of your team in high trust, elite standards, pervasive selflessness, total commitment, and accelerated learning. Most importantly, Jerry and John illuminate the vitality of love in being a champion teammate for building true teams."

—Ryan Bernacchi, Captain, USN (Ret.), former Blue Angels flight leader, Top Gun instructor, and director of Leadership and Character Development, United States Naval Academy

"Winning a championship requires more than talent. It takes a locker room with strong leadership, team unity, and a competitive fiber in every player. As coaches we often tell our athletes to be better teammates but we don't teach them how to do it. This new book from John O'Sullivan and Jerry Lynch will become your guide for teaching people how to be better teammates and the key ingredients in creating a high-performance championship-level environment."

—Caleb Porter, two-time MLS champion coach of Portland Timbers and Columbus Crew

"John and Jerry continue to lead the charge in both the purpose and the goal of what a youth sports experience can look, act, and feel like when it is done with great care, intention, and humility. They have chosen to use the word *timeless* and I couldn't agree more. In life, it is the timeless lessons that never fade, that teach us, and that are taught to the next generation. Learning how to be a great teammate transcends sports and shows up in marriages, families, relationships, careers, hobbies, and more. Connecting, leading, and competing as John and Jerry show us are timeless. Yes, you will gain knowledge, and best of all, there are immediate actions to take right now."

—*Jon Torine, Super Bowl champion strength and conditioning coach, Indianapolis Colts*

"Connecting, competing, and leading are truly an honorable way to succeed through humility. Two of our favorite quotes are, 'It is safe to speak up and make the children feel safe in our environment,' along with 'Winning externally on the scoreboard is the by-product of the victories within.' Coaching golf is our true 'calling' and *The Champion Teammate* is a guide to implement for coaches, and everyone in our daily lives. We resonate with every word and thank you, John O'Sullivan and Jerry Lynch, for bringing your insight to life for all to embrace the 'we' instead of 'me.' Bravo!"

—*Susie Redman, 2023 PGA Youth Player Development Award, former LPGA Pro*
—*Kevin Kirk, 2018 PGA Teacher of the Year Award, coach of Olympic, Ryder Cup, and Masters champion golfers*

"Jerry and John's new book *The Champion Teammate* is what the world needs now. It's right on time, for the right reasons, in the right way, by the right people. This book is who they are and what they've been offering countless teams, organizations, and individuals with much success over many decades of extraordinary work."

—*George Mumford, author of The Mindful Athlete and Unlocked: Embrace Your Greatness, Find the Flow, Discover Success*

"I have had the pleasure of working with Jerry Lynch for many years, and I know he knows what it takes to be a champion. Jerry and John have identified one of the most essential parts of creating a championship culture: helping athletes become exceptional teammates. Every championship team I have been a part of, over my 50-plus years as a lacrosse player and coach, has been full of great teammates who demonstrated the exact same traits, behaviors, and actions taught in *The Champion Teammate*. I strongly recommend their latest book to all athletes and coaches who want to create a championship culture and discover true success in their sport!"

—*Gary Gait, world champion, US and Canadian Hall of Fame, head men's lacrosse coach, Syracuse University*

THE
CHAMPION
TEAMMATE

Timeless Lessons to Connect, Compete, and Lead in Sports & Life

JERRY LYNCH AND JOHN O'SULLIVAN
Leadership, Performance and Team Culture Specialists

THE CHAMPION TEAMMATE

Timeless Lessons to Connect, Compete, and Lead in Sports & Life

ISBN: 978-1-7343426-3-5 hardback
ISBN: 978-1-7343426-2-8 paperback
ISBN: 978-1-7343426-4-2 ebook

Library of Congress Control Number: 2023908666

Changing the Game Project
60643 Thunderbird
Bend, Oregon, 97702

www.ChangingTheGameProject.com

Cover Design by: 99 Designs
Interior Design by: Laura Jones, lauraflojo.com

_____

NAME

_____

TEAM NAME

CONTENTS

PART III: LEAD

INTRODUCTION

Begin Within

As we complete the writing of our book, *The Champion Teammate*, the 2022 FIFA World Cup has just come to an end. In one of the most thrilling World Cups of all time, and, without a doubt, the greatest final ever played, Argentina defeated France to win their third world title. Led by their 35-year-old talisman Lionel Messi, who had won everything in his career except the World Cup, Argentina took a 2–0 lead in the final, were tied 2–2, went up 3–2 in overtime, were again tied, and finally prevailed in a penalty kick shootout. As Messi kissed the golden trophy and lifted it overhead, this final championship cemented his legacy for many as the greatest player of all time.

For the two of us writing this book, this FIFA World Cup provided fertile ground to look at exceptional teammates, team dynamics, optimal performance, and leadership. Teams that were not filled with superstars, such as Morocco and Croatia, made the semifinals, while star-studded teams such as Belgium, Germany, and Senegal never even got out of the group stage. What was it that allowed some groups of players to come together as a team of effective teammates, while others never quite gelled?

This gala event also provided a likely swan song not only for Lionel Messi but for his greatest foil throughout his career, 37-year-old Cristiano Ronaldo. While Messi has won seven Ballon d'Or awards, annually given to the world's best male player, Ronaldo has won five. They have each shattered scoring records for club and country, set numerous records, and hauled in dozens of league, cup, and Champions League trophies in their star-studded careers. Ronaldo's Portugal won the European Championship in 2016, while Messi and Argentina won the championship in South America in 2021. Year after year they pushed each other to new heights of excellence. All that eluded each man was a World Cup winner's medal.

While each man has kept himself in remarkable physical condition, and continues to perform at a high level, their physical skills have waned given their age. They no longer press on defense, or have the same speed as they did in their 20s. Their brilliant technique and insight have allowed them to keep playing at the highest levels, but during the 2022 World Cup, their paths diverged.

This extraordinary World Cup saw an Argentina team led by quintessential teammate Messi, surrounded by younger teammates who idolized him, spilling their blood to get him a title. It saw tactics designed to get the best out of him, and a coach who understood how Messi could best contribute. Messi scored seven goals, took home the World Cup, and solidified his legacy as a national hero.

Portugal, on the other hand, underachieved. Ronaldo reacted poorly to getting subbed in a group game. He was benched in their round 16 game, and the team played its best game of the tournament. He remained on the bench and only played the last 40 minutes of their losing quarterfinal effort, and then walked off the field without shaking hands or acknowledging the fans. This came on the heels of the recent termination of his club contract with Manchester United for similar behavior detrimental to his team. Messi was the ultimate team player and cemented his legacy; Ronaldo was a distraction, and, sadly, continued the process of tarnishing his.

We share this story to introduce our book to illustrate what it looks like to be a **champion teammate**. The 2022 World Cup poignantly game in town. Someone should tell them. It has made all the difference in the world to me."

Essential Questions

You will notice in many chapters in this book that we will ask three basic questions which will help you and your team to get the most out of your efforts:

- What do I/we need to *start* doing—that I/we are not doing—in order to . . .
- What do I/we need to *stop* doing—that I/we are currently doing—in order to . . .
- What do I/we need to *keep* doing—that I/we are currently doing—in order to . . .

These we call the essential questions, and we use them often in our work with teams on many topics. They promote excellent individual and group reflection on numerous topics, and we encourage you to use them to promote healthy team discussions whenever an issue comes up.

How to Use This Book

We have conveniently divided this guidebook into three sections: Connect, Compete, and Lead. Under each section are a series of lessons that will demonstrate how you can assume the qualities of a champion teammate. Here is a treasury of inspirational, insightful, and time-honored lessons, reflective stories, and contemplative thoughts rooted in the wisdom accrued from our global involvement with over a hundred championship teams, consultancies with Hall of Fame coaches, our *Way of Champions Podcast*, and hundreds of clinics and conferences that we conduct on the subject of being an exceptional teammate, coach, and parent. We will share stories with you of world-famous athletes and teams who epitomize each lesson, as well as wisdom garnered from

Native American tradition, ancient Eastern thought, modern-day gladiators, and Western psychology.

At the end of each chapter there is an easily usable practical section called "Optimize Your Performance," a gathering of tools, strategies, and activities you and your team can use to implement each lesson more effectively. These nuggets may suggest reading a book together, offering some questions for discussion, or related team practices that will put you in the same boat, pulling together. We also provide plenty of space on these pages to record your thoughts, write your answers, and jot down ideas you may wish to remember. The more you embrace and work this pragmatic section of the chapter, the more you will derive from this book, and the more exceptional you will be in sports and in life.

In Part I: CONNECT, we share lessons about winning the relationship game, the cornerstone of any great team culture. We teach you how to use your influence wisely, elevate those around you, and set high standards for your team. You will learn how to be a selfless giver, how to raise and lower the temperature of the group, see the experience through your teammates' eyes, and compete with joy.

In Part II: COMPETE, we give you and your teammates specific, powerful ways to, as we like to say, "compete like crazy with your hair on fire." We teach you how to Pound the Rock and Win the Day, two of our favorite concepts for competitive development. We discuss the importance of training yourself to respond instead of react, to be comfortable being uncomfortable, and to take the steps necessary to develop great habits, while breaking those that are harmful and ineffective. We teach you how to use failure as your fuel, how to practice mindfulness and visualization to prepare and overcome fear and self-doubt, and to be patient and persist along your journey.

In Part III: LEAD, there are stories that will teach you how and when to lead, and how to step aside and follow. It is here that you will learn about humility, trust, and the disaster that awaits if your team culture allows whining and complaining. It will teach you how to speak up and address any issues before they become too big, how to give everyone a role, how being grateful can elevate your entire team, and how to help you be the teammate that everyone looks to when times get tough.

This is a book that can be applied not just to sports but to all of your life. The lessons within are timeless and can be implemented in all aspects of your world. You can read it cover to cover or lesson by lesson. You can choose to read it alone or with your team in a group setting.

Take the time to discuss each topic, answer the discussion questions, digest each lesson, and implement it in your next practice or game. It is up to you. Don't be afraid to jump around based on what topic interests your group or what is most essential and imperative for everyone. If a subject or topic hits you between the eyes, let that indicate to you where you must go. But as one of our chapters suggests, "Go slowly, arrive sooner."

When you go slowly, you take these lessons intellectually from your head (knowledge) into your heart (wisdom), a mere physical eighteen inches that oftentimes feels like miles. It takes time, but it's worth it. When taken to heart it helps make the lessons learned much deeper, sturdier, and stronger, and more likely to last longer and to hold up under pressure and over time.

Today you may be reading this as a member of a sports team, but throughout your life you will be a part of many teams. These timeless lessons are usable, forever, in sports and in life. Those other life teams may be work related; they may be your family; some may be at a church, temple, or synagogue; or in a community leadership role or as part of a military group. Your life will be filled with different types of teams and teammates, and our hope is that this book serves you not just for this season, but throughout your life.

If you live the principles taught within, you will always be in demand. You will always be sought out to join influential groups. You will be more productive, and a stronger leader. You will get more accomplished in less time. And most importantly, you will know how to deal with the good times and the bad, and be far more likely to derive joy from every team you are part of for the rest of your life.

Being a champion teammate is a life-changing, transformational journey. It is a daily choice to do the right thing for you and your teammates. Every choice you make is a vote for the type of teammate and person you want to be. Eventually you rack up enough votes to solidify your new identity as an exceptional teammate and an extraordinary person.

Each choice you make will help you gain a deeper understanding of what it means to be on a high-performing team, pulling together, and seeking a common goal, something greater than any one on the team. You will have more joy and fun, and will gain more fulfillment from this than you have from any team you have ever experienced.

When you implement these lessons, coupled with having some decent physical talent, the scoreboard will likely reflect success. But even if it does not, you still will be on a meaningful and purposeful path that provides a joyful, loving experience, going into battle every day with your fellow warriors, having each other's backs. Being a champion teammate will not guarantee a championship. But all champions have exceptional teammates. Is there really an option other than taking this journey and being the extraordinary teammate that you hope to be?

"One day a teammate or coach will have a choice to recommend you, hire you or not hire you," says college football coach Keith Scott. "They will remember if you were dependable, committed, a complainer, selfish, a team player, and what you did when no one was around. Who you are today impacts you tomorrow." That is why you must start being an exceptional teammate today. We're ready to help you begin. . . . Will you join us?

If so, let's begin our journey together and learn how you can perform and succeed by being a champion teammate through your connection, competitive spirit, and leadership. Let this guidebook come through in the clutch, every time, to help you experience extraordinary joy, satisfaction, and success. Let's get after it.

Jerry Lynch
Santa Cruz, California

John O'Sullivan
Bend, Oregon

December 2022

PART I: CONNECT

Winning the Relationship Game

None of us, including me, ever do great things. But we can do small things, with great love, and together we can do something wonderful.

—Mother Teresa

The famous storyteller Aesop once wrote a tale about four oxen and a lion. A lion used to prowl an area where the four oxen lived, and the oxen became very adept at fending off the lion. When they saw the lion, they would each turn their tails toward one another, so that whatever way the lion approached from, he would be met by the horns of one of the oxen. They stuck together day after day and eventually the lion left them alone.

The four oxen made decisions together and traveled to the same places to graze, always staying safe in numbers. Every once in a while the oxen would see a lone ox enter the field, but it would soon disappear and they wondered why. One day, the oxen quarreled, and they each went their separate ways to graze. In the words of Aesop, "Then the lion attacked them one by one and soon made an end of all four."

A highly functioning team is greater than the sum of all its parts. No matter how fast, strong, or skillful someone is, great teams usually overcome great individuals over the long haul. As great as Lionel Messi is as a player, he could not win a World Cup without a team dedicated to suffering and battling together. Michael Jordan did not win a championship until he accepted that only a strong team around him could get him a ring.

There are many examples of incredible athletes who lack the committed team needed to win a championship, as well as teams filled with talent but who have not bought into a common cause, with common values, behaviors, and standards. When that happens, you are simply oxen, on your own, in a field full of lions.

Connection is the single greatest force that can bring your team together and help it endure the hardship, suffering, and commitment to win a championship. Love is the most powerful force in your ability to win the relationship game. When we use the word *love*, we describe that unbreakable bond that you feel among close friends, family, and great teams. It is the deep respect, loyalty, and affection that holds you together through thick and thin. Without love, and all that comes with it, you will never be greater than the sum of your parts.

Part I of this book is about the connection that great teams build through the type of love described above. We chose CONNECT to be the first of the three divisions of this book because without a strong foundation of love, there is no leadership or competitiveness. Winning the relationship game is the key that makes all else work.

What separates the relationship masters from relationship disasters? It is the day-to-day intentional action to establish strong interpersonal connections, which is the key to opening the door to successful team cultures. What we offer in Part I are concepts that are the ultimate, science-based, practical guides to deeper connection, caring, and love. Why is this so important? Keep reading.

Strong, connected relationships enable others to buy into the culture and go the distance competitively. Exceptional teammates demonstrate their love and respect for each other, their club, and their school. This kind of connection is about establishing high standards, elevating those around you, and being a teammate who can turn the temperature up and down. In Part I, you will learn how important it is to give, not get; to catch your teammates being good; and to recognize that your influence is never, ever neutral. When these elements occur, you win the all-important relationship game.

"None of us, including me, ever do great things," said Mother Teresa. "But we can do small things, with great love, and together we can do something wonderful." Put love at the center of all you do, and repeatedly demonstrate your love, and wonderful things will happen this season. Let's go!

1. Be an Elevator

The more we care for the happiness of others, the greater is our own sense of well-being. Cultivating a close, warm-hearted feeling for others automatically puts the mind at ease. It is the ultimate source of success in life.

—The Dalai Lama

Many years ago Jerry was working at the University of North Carolina with the women's lacrosse and volleyball teams, and he had an encounter that changed his life and taught him the essence of what it means to be an elevator to those around you. One day following a practice, he had the chance to meet his idol, men's basketball coach Dean Smith. To say he was nervous is a massive understatement. As Jerry walked into his office and asked the receptionist if he could make an appointment to meet Coach Smith on his next visit, she strongly said, "No way. He'll love to see you . . . I will get him now."

This raised Jerry's anxiety even more as he felt ill prepared for such a meeting. Within minutes Coach Smith walked out, looked him in the eyes and said, "What an honor to meet you Dr. Lynch. I have been hearing about all the good things you have been doing with our teams." Immediately this humble, authentic, vulnerable person insisted on making Jerry feel important, valued, empowered, respected, and relevant. In fact, Coach Smith made him feel like he was the most important person in his life at that moment. He was demonstrating what a true elevator leader is. As Jerry says to this day, "I would have done anything for him had he asked. I would have licked the dust off the floor of the basketball court." Jerry was so inspired and empowered by him that within the next year he wrote and published a book, *Coaching with Heart*, in Coach Smith's honor.

The lesson Jerry learned was how "feelings equal function." This concept is science-based, tried and tested over the years, and is quite effective in creating functional environments in team cultures. When you feel pessimistic, unimportant, devalued, unloved, weak, fearful, and needy, your performance will suffer that day. If you feel optimistic, important, valued, loved, strong, fearless, and abundant, your confidence and performance will soar. In honor of Coach Smith, we continue to this day to find ways to elevate others in our lives, noticing the impact we have as Coach Smith did with Jerry years ago. And, as a great teammate, you can do this too and make a huge difference with your teammates.

Breaking down the wisdom of the Dalai Lama from the opening quote, to be a high-impact teammate, you must cultivate a close, connective, and caring relationship with all of those in your circle, including the team, staff, and athletes. When you lift up your teammates, you become emotionally elevated as well. When an entire group feels really good about each other, everyone performs at a higher level. And, ultimately, this is what we all desire.

So the choice is yours. Think less of yourself, or think of yourself less and more about those on your team. Being an elevator is a conscious decision about focusing more on *giving* to others rather than on *getting* from them. Begin by giving them the opportunity to feel really good about themselves, and then step back and notice how they perform, act, work, compete, and behave. Notice, as well, the collateral benefit, which is how you feel having given from your heart in this way.

There is an ancient Buddhist expression: "From little streams come big rivers." In other words, when you take the time to be mindful about your teammates and elevate their emotional state, it is a small gesture, yet the outcomes of such action are enormous. Almost like magic, you'll begin to witness your team being super willing and eager to give back to all by going the distance when the coaches ask them to go all out. There will be a greater sense of cohesion and unity in a cooperative and collaborative effort to contribute more to the mission of the team. Your small positive comments influence huge changes and outcomes, like being more loyal, competing with more intensity, increasing the overall work ethic of the group, and developing a safe environment where all can have less fear and be mentally tougher.

We have developed an easy-to-implement strategy to help you elevate your teammates. Many teams we work with have used this strategy extensively. It is called the RIVER Effect. RIVER is an acronym which stands for Relevant, Inspired, Valued, Empowered, and Respected. When used properly, it will change the environment to one that is more connective, caring, productive, and cooperative.

Your job as a champion teammate is to marinate others in the RIVER. It is simple and easy when you stay mindful of catching others doing something right, something good, something that contributes to the overall team mission of being the best you can be, at practice, at an event, or in life. Here are a few examples that you can use to help elevate your teammates and have them appreciate you more. Use your ingenuity to create other positive RIVER statements.

RELEVANT: Hey, Jack, you are important to this team. We love your efforts.

INSPIRE: Megan, if you keep playing with that intensity, you'll be one of the best on the team.

VALUE: Josh, we all value your presence on the team. You model being a great teammate.

3.   What do you specifically need to *start* doing—that you are not doing—to be an elevator?

_____

_____

_____

4.   What do you specifically need to *stop* doing—that you are currently doing—to be a better elevator?

_____

_____

_____

5. What team member is difficult to be with and how can you be a positive influence to help?

_____

_____

_____

6. With your team, discuss how we can use the RIVER Effect to elevate the performance of our teammates. Do we want to share a RIVER comment after every practice? After every game?

_____

_____

_____

2. Set Standards, Not Rules

Most people naturally play to one thing, and that is winning.
Playing to a standard is the biggest secret to our success.

—Dave Brandt,
six-time NCAA champion coach,
Messiah College men's soccer

Discipline yourself, so others don't have to.

—John Wooden,
10-time NCAA champion coach,
UCLA men's basketball

Messiah College is a small Christian college in Mechanicsburg, Pennsylvania, about twelve miles from Harrisburg. The school is known for its liberal arts education and its evangelical Christian faith, and their sports programs compete at the NCAA Division III level. Since the year 2000, the Messiah College men's soccer team has won eleven NCAA Division III Championships, and the women's team has won six titles.

Messiah also holds the distinction of being the only NCAA soccer program to win both the men's and women's title the same year, a feat they have accomplished four times. Their continued success led Michael Zigarelli, a professor of leadership and strategy at Messiah, to examine the underpinnings of this championship program and led to his 2011 book *The Messiah Method: The Seven Disciplines of the Winningest College Soccer Program in America.*

In the book, Zigarelli quotes former Messiah head coach Dave Brandt on the idea of standards vs. rules. "Most people naturally play to one thing, and that is winning," says Brandt. "Playing to a standard is the biggest secret to our success." If you have the opportunity to speak with athletes who have played at Messiah, they speak about this high standard that permeates the program. They talk about the competitiveness of every single session. They speak about coming in for preseason and not wanting to let their teammates down by being unfit or not making the team's fitness standards. They talk about repeating activities in practice time again and again to get them right. They speak about training late nights in January, a full eight months before the season starts, and trying to stretch their advantage over other programs a little further.

Most importantly, they all speak about "leaving the shirt in a better place" by doing all the little things to get better every single day. That is why Messiah has set such a standard of excellence and year after year return to final fours and win national championships. It is a standard that many others are beginning to emulate.

One of the most important things we have learned on our coaching journey is the importance of establishing standards for your program, instead of numerous rules. Rules are something to be broken. Standards are there to be aspired to. Many teams make a bunch of rules and hope standards emerge, but you will be far more successful if you set high standards and encourage your teammates to try and reach them.

What we have learned through experience and by studying some of the world's best coaches and winningest programs is that consistently great teams have very few rules and very high standards. They are as intentional in establishing team standards as they are about fitness, tactics, and technical development. They do not leave these things to chance. We have also learned that if we try to establish lots of rules instead of standards, our coaches, captains, and team leadership end up acting like policemen, constantly chasing down rule breakers instead of setting a high standard to be aspired to.

To be clear, a *rule* is a regulation or guideline, while a *standard* is a level of quality. Rules can be demeaning because they are all about control. When young athletes encounter rules, they constantly test them to see how far they can go before they are held accountable for breaking them. Endless sets of rules can be exhausting to enforce and can cripple a coach's or captain's ability to make decisions on an individual basis.

Standards, on the other hand, are inspiring. They are something to strive for and attain. They result in growth, as athletes hold each other accountable for reaching higher instead of sinking to the level of a rule. Standards are levels of achievement that the whole group buys into and pushes each other toward, and are usually policed within the group. In a nutshell, rules have a negative connotation—don't break me or else—while standards are far more positive: live up to me, and you will be your best self.

John currently continues to coach youth soccer, and one of the first things he does with his teams, whether they are eight or eighteen years old, is establish standards. When we consult with teams on the collegiate level, the first thing we do is establish standards. These are the principles we are going to live by on and off the field or the court, as well as the values that we are all willing to hold each other accountable for. Great teammates aspire to live up to the standards we set. They are not perfect, and of course at times fall short. But the standard does not change for them, and is always there to be aspired to.

Think about it this way. Here are a set of rules:

- Be in bed by 10 p.m.
- Don't eat dessert at meals.
- Be off your electronic devices one hour before bed.

Each of these things is something that will help our team perform, no doubt. But who is going to police them? The coach? The captains? Are you going to knock on doors every night and check screen time on people's phones? And how do we punish rule breakers? Fines? Suspensions? Our team becomes a police state.

On the other hand, here is a team standard:

- Live a healthy lifestyle that will optimize your performance on and off the field.

Does this not encompass all these rules around proper sleep and nutrition? Doesn't it ask the same of our team, but does so in an aspirational way? We are still asked to make good choices and develop good habits, and we are doing so NOT to avoid being punished but to avoid letting our teammates down! Love, lead, and compete to high standards, and hold your teammates accountable for doing the same, and you will not only be an exceptional teammate, but you will have an extraordinary team.

Optimize Your Performance

1. Discuss the story of Messiah College Soccer: In groups, discuss the story of Messiah soccer and the concept of playing to a standard. How does this relate to your team at the moment? Does your group have rules or standards or a mix of both? What do you look like when you are competing your very best? What do you have to *start* doing to compete this way more consistently? What do you have to *stop* doing to compete this way more often? What do you need to *keep* doing? Write down your takeaways here.

_____

_____

_____

_____

_____

2. The 20-Minute Team Standards Exercise: Sit your team down and ask them to list the qualities of a great teammate. Put it up on a whiteboard or clipboard, and once you have your list, have everyone sign it below the statement "I commit to being the type of teammate described above." Refer to this every day, and have a daily standard at each practice. Write down your takeaways here.

_____

_____

_____

_____

_____

_____

3. The 90-Minute Team Standards Exercise: Similar to the exercise above, have everyone on your team come up with three words that describe a great teammate. Then have everyone share their words as you compile a list on a whiteboard. See which words come up the most, combine similar ones, and you will come up with three to five standards that mean the most to your team. Then break into groups and have each group define what that standard means for your group; what it looks like in practice, games, and off the field; and what it gets you when you uphold it. Put these up in your locker room, on shirts, or even come up with a team slogan that encapsulates all you stand for. (Note: Some of our chapter titles work well.) Write down your takeaways here.

_____

_____

_____

_____

_____

culture and led UMD to four national championships while being recognized as the best lacrosse athlete of all time up to that point.

What kind of influence do you have? You must understand that as a teammate your influence, as Tony Robbins says in the above quote, is the single most important skill you can master. And may we add, your influence is never neutral. You can light up the lives of others or cast them into darkness. Your influence is either positive or negative in every situation, and you want to master the art of having a positive influence on your teammates.

To be a positive influence on the lives of your teammates is a blessing not just for them but for you as well. As the opening quote implies, regardless of your role on the team, having a positive influence on teammates practically assures you a place on the bus. No matter how many points, goals, hits, or assists, your greatness will always be intimately aligned with your ability to affect your teammates positively. A great teammate affects others forever. You never can tell how wide and far your influence goes.

In the brilliant words of poet Maya Angelou, we all need to "try to be a rainbow in someone's cloud." Your body language, tone, expressions, gestures, and words all have an impact on how things transpire. So does your behavior. One of Jerry's favorite things to do when he meets a team is to run up a hill together. By doing so, he demonstrates his willingness to experience what they do in training and therefore influence them by example.

Ancient generals were considered influential because they were willing to experience the same heat, cold, toil, hunger, thirst, and danger as their soldiers and were respected and admired because of this influential behavior. When Jerry enters a room full of coaches and athletes, he walks with a bounce, stands straight, keeps his head up, looks others in the eye, and smiles. His influence is palpable, sending the message that things are under control, all is fine, it's all OK. As a champion teammate, the more often you become aware of the power of your influence, the more you have a say in the direction your teammates go, what they do, and how they feel. It is that simple.

When Jerry is coaching one of his teams, he usually begins the sessions by inviting the athletes to "huddle up" close, forming a tight series of concentric circles around him (assuming there are 25 or so athletes on the team). This communicates togetherness, kindness, oneness, connectedness, and, most importantly, a sense of goodness. Then Jerry says the following: "I love being here. I love being with you. There's not another place I'd rather be or another group of athletes I'd rather be with at this moment than with you." This spoken truth is visibly felt deeply by the entire group. They truly believe he cares, and he really does. He often will touch a shoulder and establish good eye contact with one person. Being aware of this power to influence others is something you as a good teammate need to know. Your teammates will love it. By doing this, you set a positive, heart-directed, caring tone for all the good work the entire team will then do together.

Always be aware of your influence. When we all demonstrate caring, positive action we help create a team that is united, connected, and cohesive. Your influence as a teammate is never neutral. The more aware of your influence you are, the more powerful it is. What do you wish it to be?

Optimize Your Performance

1. Answer these questions and act accordingly:

   a. What do you need to *start* doing—that you are currently not doing—in order to demonstrate the power of your influence in a positive way?

   _____

   _____

   _____

   b. What do you need to *stop* doing—that you are currently doing—in order to demonstrate the power of your influence in a positive way?

   _____

   _____

   _____

3. MASTER YOUR INFLUENCE

c. What do you need to *keep* doing—that you are currently doing—to use your influence in a positive way?

_____

_____

_____

2. In your group, share a story of an athlete using their influence to bring about positive change in competition and in the community, just as Jen Adams did for the University of Maryland. How did they do it? Why does this matter?

_____

_____

_____

3. Here is a simple checklist to remind you how to have a positive influence as a teammate. Put a check next to the items that you consistently do.

☐ Balance critical comments with supportive ones.
☐ Avoid arguments, if possible, and choose your battles.
☐ Praise all the good someone does.
☐ Apologize when you are wrong.
☐ Let others talk as you listen.
☐ Ask a teammate something about their family or what's keeping them busy.
☐ Call them by name.
☐ Be present and look in their eyes.
☐ Help out when help is needed.
☐ Be kind and nonjudgmental.
☐ Bathe others in the RIVER.

4. Be a Thermostat, Not a Thermometer

Act as if what you do makes a difference. It does.

—William James

The great FC Barcelona teams from 2008–2016 were some of the greatest teams of all time, in any sport. They won multiple league, cup and Champions League titles, including all six competitions they entered in 2009 (Copa Del Rey, La Liga, Champions League, Spanish Super Cup, European Super Cup, FIFA Club World Cup). They played extraordinary soccer, and the team was filled with superstars such as Lionel Messi, Xavi, Andrés Iniesta, Neymar, and others. The captain of those teams was Carles Puyol.

Puyol was a product of Barcelona's famed La Masia Academy and had grown up with many of the team's star players. He was not a flashy headliner like the others. He was a gritty defender. He did the dirty work, covered for others, made huge defensive plays, and led through his work ethic and inspirational attitude. He was the glue that held the egos in check, and though his top traits rarely made the stats sheet, without him Barcelona would have never achieved great heights.

Puyol was a leader, a warrior, and humble at the same time. He captained teams with stars such as Messi, Neymar, and Ronaldinho, and more-famous teammates often called him the best professional they had ever been around. If you google "Carles Puyol leadership," you will find highlight videos of Puyol asking teammates to stop over-the-top celebrations that humiliated an opponent, or to quit complaining about or playacting for a foul. In one instance, he gets slapped by an opposing player, and then intervenes and pushes his own teammates away before a shoving match can start, taking the temperature down and keeping their focus on the game. Puyol is the ultimate thermostat, when many others are simply thermometers.

We have all been part of a competition, or a season, when things go sideways for the group. It might be a poor call by an official, or it might be a bad run of form, but all of a sudden everyone in the group loses their head, or starts to play tight, tense, and tentative. These are the moments we need thermostats, not thermometers. And while these two things seem to be very similar—something to do with temperature—they do very different things.

As you all know, thermometers take the temperature of a room. Sometimes it is hot, sometimes it is cold, and they reflect exactly what is going on. Many teams can get stuck in thermometer mode, reflecting what is happening in the moment or during that stage of the season. If one person is low energy, soon the whole group is. If one person loses their head or conflict arises, soon everyone is sucked into the drama.

The problem with many teams, and leaders, is that they act like thermometers. The culture of the group goes up and down based upon the temperature of the day, which leads to inconsistency and lack of identity or the inability to change things when they are going south. Next thing you know, you have lost a competition you should have won, or blown a conference championship, because of a couple of bad games.

Thermostats, on the other hand, adjust the temperature. If it is too hot, thermostats bring the temperature down, and if it is too cold, they bump up the heat a bit. Great teams, and great leaders, are more like thermostats. They recognize when something is not right, and they adjust. No energy in practice? They have the courage to bump it up a notch. Negativity and cliques arising? They bring that to an end quickly by addressing the issue when it is small.

If team members are losing focus, thermostats help everyone around them get dialed back in. Teams in thermostat mode know what the temperature needs to be, as defined by their culture and values, and they adjust accordingly. When these teams adjust the temperature, it isn't done to call anyone out or shame anyone; it is done because the team has agreed to abide by these standards and values. When you act as a thermostat, you are demonstrating your love for each other, and sometimes that love needs to be tough love. This is a sign of respect.

Sadly, some teammates can be thermostats in the wrong way, turning down the temperature and sucking the energy out of a positive team by whining, complaining, and gossiping. These things are like vomit; the person doing them feels better and everyone else around feels worse. When you complain, whine, and gossip, no one says, "I am so glad I was a part of that, I cannot wait to hear them do that again." It doesn't achieve or improve anything, especially for the person doing the complaining. Your performance and your standing on your team will improve the moment you stop complaining.

Thermometers are nice to have on a team when things are going well, but thermostats are a necessity so we don't get too high or too low. Thermometers are about reacting, and thermostats are about responding. Thermometers are about being a victim of our circumstances, and thermostats are about intentionality, realizing that we always have a choice to respond and not to react. Being a thermometer is easy; being a thermostat takes courage. Average teams are populated with thermometers, but championship teams are full of thermostats.

Which one are you? What about your team?

Every season, and every competition, is filled with thermometer and thermostat moments. If we want to get better every day, we need to have the courage to be in thermostat mode. When an opponent goes on a run, we need to know what is needed to stop it. When there is a bad call or a bad bounce and we lose focus, we need to adjust and get it back.

When practice is not at the required standard, we must demonstrate our love, reset our focus quickly, and be a thermostat. Dial it up a bit out of love for your teammates. Condemn the behaviors that are not helping you grow as a team, or you are in effect condoning them. Have a bad moment, but don't string together a bunch of them.

That's what thermostats do. If we can be thermostats this season, we can do great things.

Optimize Your Performance

1. Rate yourself on a scale of 1–5, where 1 is a thermometer who goes along with the current temperature of the group, and 5 is a thermostat like Carles Puyol, who raises and lowers it as needed. Think about the moments of highest stress (down on the scoreboard, after a bad call, etc.) because these moments are when it matters most.

   _____

   _____

2. Gather with your teammates and rate your team on a scale of 1–5. Then break into groups and have a discussion around the following questions:

   a. Describe a difficult moment for our team when we all reacted in a poor manner, when we needed to be thermostats and instead acted like thermometers.

   _____

   _____

b. What could we have done differently in that moment? Who could have stepped up and changed the temperature?

_____

_____

_____

c. Describe a moment when we responded to a difficult situation and acted like thermostats instead of thermometers. What did we do that worked well? How can we do that more often?

_____

_____

_____

d. Bonus: Have everyone anonymously write down the three thermostats on your team and compile the results.

_____

_____

_____

3. Coaches, consider selecting your team captains on a thermostat vs. thermometer basis, using some of the criteria from this rating. Would this help your team?

_____

_____

_____

5. Give Selflessly

Our players' selfish acts can poison a locker room. Basketball is a
team game about unselfish acts that result in team building.
—Coach Dean Smith, University of North Carolina

One of Jerry's favorite coaches that he has worked with over the years
is Steve Kerr of the Golden State Warriors. He won five NBA Championships as a player and has now won four as a coach. When Kerr
took over the helm as head coach with the Warriors organization, one
of his first acts was to talk with Andre "Iggy" Iguodala about his role as
a teammate. Iggy was an NBA all-star and consistent starter on every
team he played on throughout his career, yet Kerr asked how he would
feel coming off the bench when needed for the good of the team. Iggy
unselfishly responded that he would agree to do whatever is best for
the team. He trusted Kerr and gave to his team in this way all season.
The Warriors reached the NBA Finals that season, and the coaching
staff decided to tweak the lineup. Iggy was suddenly called upon to
start. And here is the best part of the story. His phenomenal performances throughout the series earned him the NBA Finals MVP, and
the Warriors won their first championship under Kerr.

Selflessness is the unconditional willingness to put the team before
your individual needs. There is never a guarantee that you'll get something back in return, but you do it anyway because that is a reward in
itself. Iggy did just that. He was, and continues to be, emblematic of

what we call the champion teammate. Though not expected or guaranteed, in the end his giving was rewarded with getting. Iggy embraced his role to such an extent that years later, when he wrote his autobiography, he titled it *The Sixth Man*.

It only takes one mindless teammate demonstrating selfish acts on a consistent basis to completely destroy a positive team culture. When you see this happening, the issue must be addressed, preferably by peers expressing their concerns. As a champion teammate, you may have to suggest that this conversation takes place. That is one important way that you can demonstrate being a valued and important teammate. And there are other ways to be a giver, not a getter.

We have noticed over the years how athletes are fearful of not getting something they feel they deserve. Athletes often ask the internal question, "What can I get?" In sports, we often expect to get things such as playing time, to play our favorite position, to wear our favorite number, to try hard when we feel like it, and things of that nature. These things never bring a championship; they only bring division and disharmony.

The exceptional teammate insists on asking, "How can I give?" We can give things such as our best effort every time, our willingness to play whatever position best helps our team, our complete focus, and a positive attitude day after day. This is the difference between being selfish and being selfless. An exceptional teammate is selfless, helping everyone on the team to reach higher levels of performance, joy, and satisfaction. Such a value helps to bring out your best as well as your teammates'. And you will notice that sustained, consistent selflessness becomes its own reward. When you lift others, you are often uplifted yourself. As you become a self-sacrificing, kind, and generous teammate, your teammates do as well. You begin to compete for each other and something bigger than the game itself.

We understand that it is not easy to be selfless in today's world. Sports cultures are usually about "me" rather than "we." Getting buy-in from everyone in the culture is a struggle. Most of us are afraid we will not have enough. We live our lives in fear of not getting what we believe we're entitled to. Being an exceptional teammate demands that you take the lead and expect that others will follow. We can report that when an athlete is being a good teammate and serves the interest of the team over self, others do begin to give and serve their teammates.

In his book *Man's Search for Meaning*, Viktor Frankl gives us a vivid, dramatic example of what being selfless means. While incarcerated in a Nazi death camp, Frankl noticed that those who kept their strength and sanity the longest were not those who managed by cleverness to get more than their share of scarce food. Rather, it was those who shared and gave selflessly to others the little food they had. He mentioned how those who gave to others strengthened their physical and mental condition through their selfless and kind behavior. This is what happens when champion teammates adopt this important virtue.

Exceptional teammates are givers. Once you decide to give, you will stand out. You will be a difference maker. And you will be recognized as an amazing teammate, which is actually quite a reward in and of itself.

Optimize Your Performance

To implement the virtue of selflessness, you can try the following:

1. What can you *start* doing—that you are currently not doing— to be a more selfless teammate?

_____

_____

_____

2. What can you *stop* doing—that you are currently doing—to be a more selfless teammate?

_____

_____

_____

3.   Choose one specific way that you will give to the team this week.
     Perhaps it is picking up the balls after practice, carrying the
     ball bag to the game, giving praise to others on the team, or
     helping another teammate with skill development. Simply do
     it and let others observe your generosity. By modeling the act
     of giving, your team will be more inclined to follow your kind,
     selfless behavior and become givers themselves. Notice how
     good it feels to contribute.

     _____

     _____

4.   Go to your coach and ask how you can give more to the team.
     How can you help your teammates to elevate their level of
     competing? Is there anything you can do to help make this a
     better team?

     _____

     _____

5. Discuss the story of Andre "Iggy" Iguodala with your team. How can our team learn from his example and find ways to give instead of getting?

_____

_____

_____

6. Have Love in Your Soul

It takes a number of critical factors to win an NBA championship. But if a team doesn't have the most essential ingredient—LOVE— nothing else matters.

—Phil Jackson, 11-time NBA champion coach

One of the most important lessons we teach teams is the value of practicing love as a good teammate. Many years ago, Jerry was working with a major Division I NCAA football program, and he brought his two sons, ages 9 and 7, with him. He walked into a large auditorium filled with 80 huge athletes, 13 coaches, and his sons. His very first action was to invite two team members to join him in the front so he could ask these two towering six-foot-six, 275-pound giants if they loved one another. This produced an outburst of laughter and an uproar from them and the rest of the room. No one in the room was ready for that, and Jerry knew they wouldn't be. After all, how many young men like that discuss love, with a stranger no less?

When the room got quiet, Jerry lowered his voice and said to them, "Do you see those two little kids up there in the back? If you would ever harm them in any way, I would rip off your heads." The athletes were incredulous that Jerry, a five-foot-seven skinny runner, could say and do this, and their faces had the expression of enormous fright.

He told the team that he was the dad of these two youngsters, he loved them deeply, and he would do anything to protect them at any time. He then mentioned that this was why it was important to have love for your team if you wanted to be a great teammate.

Jerry explained that when you have that kind of unrelenting, nonnegotiable, deep love for your teammates, no opponent would be able to hurt you. You may not win the game, but your opponent would have to bleed to beat you.

A light bulb went on, and the team carried that feeling of connection over to Saturday's game as they crushed an opponent that, on paper, was the better team. Love carries the day.

To be an exceptional teammate, you must love your team. There will be times when you do not like some of them, or you disapprove of their behaviors, but overall, having love in your heart is what will make you the best possible teammate.

The world's most successful collegiate soccer coach, Anson Dorrance of the University of North Carolina women's dynasty, talks about the importance of love as a core value in his 22-time national championship culture. He refers to his players as champion teammates because "we care about each other as human beings." In his classic book *The Vision of a Champion,* he alludes to this element of love by pointing out how his athletes become good teammates by being nonjudgmental, inclusive, and embracing each other in love. He talks about their sense of humanity, with no elitist separation by academics, social class, race, religion, or sexual preferences. They truly love each other and demonstrate this each day.

In the championship culture created by Cindy Timchal at the University of Maryland women's lacrosse program, the love for each other as teammates was palpable. The teams rode on the back of love to seven consecutive national championships. Working with them during these years is when Jerry became convinced that to be a great teammate, you had to love your team. The team even had a chant that they would recite before every practice and game that acknowledged "we love each other."

Since those days, Jerry has experienced over one hundred championship teams and every one of them had extraordinary love for each other. The best teammates demonstrated that love each day, empowering their teammates to reach greater heights athletically, academically, and personally. When a teammate has this love factor, barriers are torn down and connection happens. Loyalty, inspiration, and empowerment are the result of this most extraordinary success strategy—love.

Truth be known, your teammates don't care about how much you know; they just want to know how much you care. They can feel when you are annoyed, frustrated, disappointed, and turned off by some teammates. But you can still love them. The more difficult teammates are harder to love, but you must understand this: You love them not for what they do but for who they are—human beings whose intentions are pure. Their actions and behaviors that you dislike reflect their insecurity, immaturity, and fear. If you can remember this, you will be more patient with them. When you are, they will be more inclined to change the way they are being. It all comes from love and acceptance.

The best way to show your love is simple. To paraphrase Kahlil Gibran, hard work is love made visible.

Optimize Your Performance

1. How does the football story above influence how you want to treat your teammates? Have a discussion around the impact that love can have on your team.

_____

_____

2. Answer the following questions in small groups and then share with your team.

    a. What can you *start* doing—that you are currently not doing—to be a more loving teammate?

_____

_____

_____

b. What can you *stop* doing—that you are currently doing—to be a more loving teammate?

_____

_____

c. What can you *keep* doing—that you are currently doing—to be a more loving teammate?

_____

_____

d. What makes me you feel loved as a teammate and how can you give that to your team?

_____

_____

e. Which athletes demonstrate love for your team? What specifically do these athletes do that expresses their love for the team? How can you imitate this?

_____

_____

_____

3. Here are a couple of ways to demonstrate love for your teammates:

    a. Remember that love is a verb. It requires action on top of feelings. Demonstrate love by using strategies from the section called "Be an Elevator."

    b. To show love, know that "hard work is love made visible." Make a sign out of that quote, stick it on your locker room wall, and get after it!

    c. Catch teammates doing something right and acknowledge them for it.

    d. Send a teammate a positive text or email.

7. Walk in Another's Shoes

Compassion is not a virtue—it is a commitment. It's not something we have or don't have—it's something we choose to practice.

—Brené Brown, PhD, author of *Dare to Lead*

A distinguished Zen master was holding a meditation retreat of several weeks' duration, with students coming from all over Japan to attend. During one of these gatherings, a student was caught stealing. The master heard of the theft and others demanded that the student be thrown out, but the wise teacher ignored the matter. Later, that same student was caught stealing again, and once more the Zen master ignored the complaint. The students became angry and drew up a petition to have the student removed or they would leave in protest.

When the master read the petition, he called them all before him. "You are all wise brothers," he told them. "You all know the difference between what is right and what is not right. You may leave and go somewhere else to study if you wish, but this poor brother doesn't know right from wrong. If I don't teach him, who will? I am going to keep him here even if you all leave." A flood of tears fell like a waterfall down the face of the brother who had taken their things. He lost the desire to ever steal again.

Let's use this lesson in sports.

One of the core values of the four-time NBA Champion Golden State Warriors is compassion. Coach Steve Kerr has said that the most

61

powerful leaders and cultures in the world are the ones who have an awareness of compassion for others. Being an exceptional teammate means you must be a powerful leader and, therefore, have compassion for another. Compassion could very well be the ultimate source of your success as an extraordinary teammate in sports and in life.

Simply defined, compassion is the willingness to walk in the shoes of another, specifically your teammates' and coaches'. It is a state of heart that can be taught and, therefore, learned through consistent intentional practice. It is a "heart-set" of wanting others to feel free, happy, confident, successful, and healed. Isn't this what we all crave for each other?

Coach Phil Jackson believes that this core value was an integral aspect of his leadership as a teammate with the New York Knicks and as an NBA coach. He considered it an essential element for his championship cultures with the Chicago Bulls and Los Angeles Lakers. When Michael Jordan and Kobe Bryant learned to be compassionate teammates, they transformed their teams into two of the greatest franchises of all time. If Michael and Kobe could learn the value of compassion and use it effectively, then so can you on your journey to becoming a mindful, champion teammate.

In his best seller *Sacred Hoops,* Phil talks about the importance of being a good teammate by treating those on your team with the same care you would want for yourself. When you do this, you begin to understand empathically the struggles, desires, and dreams of your teammates. With this mindful awareness, you will feel part of something bigger than yourself, and you will discover that compassion is, indeed, another nonnegotiable element for being the ultimate teammate.

The Chinese ancient book of leadership *Tao Te Ching,* states that "leaders whose positions are lasting are those who are most compassionate." Such an idea is extremely relevant for you working at being the best teammate you can be. Compassionate leaders have courage and model that with their teams. Compassion helps you to worry less about mistakes, failure, and loss, knowing that others will understand because they fail as well. With the virtue of compassion, you will empower your teammates to be brave, fearless, tenacious, and relentless because, as everyone knows, we all fail, we all make mistakes, and we will learn from them.

The value of having compassion as an element of being a great teammate in a champion culture is eloquently expressed in the wisdom of Missy Foote, a brilliant four-time national champion women's lacrosse coach at Middlebury College in Vermont:

> The most important quality of a good teammate is to value another's differences. We each bring our unique selves as we work together toward a common goal of being our very best, individually and collectively. We must have compassion with regard to our differences and remember we are all imperfect humans.

Being a great teammate also demands that you not forget about having self-compassion. Do you constantly judge yourself, compare yourself to others, or hold yourself to unreasonable standards or to other people's expectations? Do you beat yourself up or put yourself down? If any of this is true, know that without self-compassion, it is unreasonable to expect that you could have compassion for others. It all begins with loving yourself. To do this, start holding yourself a bit more lightly. Refuse to take yourself so seriously. Smile to yourself right now and laugh at being this way. There is only one you in the world, and you must cherish your uniqueness. When you practice self-compassion, it is liberating. You feel less stressed and more relaxed and energetic.

The Chinese symbol for compassion depicts a generosity of the heart, followed by an active eagerness to participate in the joy or sorrow of another. For a practical example, see number 2 in the section below.

Optimize Your Performance

1. How can you apply the Zen master story to your development as a teammate? How can we best show compassion for the journey our teammates are on? Discuss in small groups and then share with the team.

   _____

   _____

   _____

2. When in the company of your teammates, ask yourself this question internally: "How do my teammates feel right now, physically, emotionally, and mentally?" When you find the answer, initiate a conversation with anyone who seems receptive to discussing what matters to them at this moment.

   _____

   _____

   _____

3. After a big victory, ask yourself this question in your head: "How do our opponents feel right now?" Then share what you believe to be their feelings with your teammates. This will demonstrate care and concern for the opponent who showed up and helped you to discover how good you can be. You can celebrate your victory AND have compassion for others at the same time.

    _____

    _____

4. What do you need to *start* doing—that you are not currently doing—to practice compassion?

    _____

    _____

    _____

5. What do you need to *stop* doing—that you are currently doing—to practice compassion?

_____

_____

_____

8. Embrace Investment Season

Opportunity is missed by most people because it is dressed
in overalls and looks like work.

—Thomas Edison

For every collegiate sports program in the United States, the COVID pandemic in 2020 resulted in canceled, postponed, and completely disrupted seasons. Spring sports had their seasons canceled by March and fall sports, outside of football, had their seasons delayed into spring of 2021. For many athletes the last opportunity to compete at a collegiate level vanished, and for others it was an opportunity to reflect upon whether sports were still as important to them, given all the world was enduring. For a third group, though, the pandemic became an opportunity to invest.

For one of the NCAA teams that John was working with, spring was their usual off-season, and they had no idea how long it would last and when they might practice or play again. It was like training for a marathon, but you did not know the date of the race. How much should we do? How can we get better? How do you peak when you do not know the date by which you are trying to be in top condition mentally and physically? As the team sat in their respective homes, scattered across the globe, they pulled together a team Zoom to check in on everyone and decide what they wanted to do moving forward.

The conversation was an honest one. The team was very good, a perennial Top 20 team but not quite Top 10 or Top 5. They knew they had to close the gap with the teams above them if they were going to compete for a conference and a national championship. This would require better physical preparation, technical development, and an overall increase in game intelligence to compete with the best of the best. The questions on that Zoom were "Are we all in? Will we use this time as the off-season, or as an investment season?"

"Investment season" was the unanimous response. So they got to work. As the players worked individually on their fitness and technical skills, coaches and leaders set up accountability groups. They also came together at least once a month to check in and to make sure everyone was doing OK. The group did fun competitions and activities to keep themselves unburdened yet focused. Day after day the team closed the gap, knowing that they were putting in more work than many of their opponents. And when they finally got to have their fall 2020 season in the spring of 2021, the fruits of their labor were evident. They beat teams they had never defeated before, and finished the season ranked #7 in the NCAA RPI. A year later this same team hit #1. Average teammates look forward to the off-season. Elite ones rest, recover, recharge, and then get after it during investment season.

Investment season is not simply an individual investment in your game or ability. It is also time to work on every single one of these relationship-building principles we have discussed in Part I of this book. It is a time to come together in small groups and hold our teammates accountable for improving, as they do the same for us. It is about building upon our strengths and our areas for improvement. The more we do this together, the more inspired and motivated we each become to put in the work. No one wants to let their teammates down, and investment season is the best time to show your teammates how much you love them. Hard work is love made visible.

Dom Starsia is the four-time NCAA champion coach of the University of Virginia men's lacrosse team. He recently wrote an article for *Inside Lacrosse* magazine in which he discussed his first championship team in 1999, a team he called the hardest-working team he ever coached. What impressed him most was the work they put in during their investment season, and how much faith it took to put in that level of work when they had no idea whether it would pay off. "The willingness to work harder every day and to engage in a complicated discussion to manage behavior away from the locker room proved to be the formula required of that team for success," wrote Starsia. "No one knew that beforehand, however, and the commitments made in fall and winter could not guarantee a championship in spring. What it did was give us a chance. . . . The commitment comes first, then (maybe) the reward. You need to convince yourself and your teammates that this leap of faith is worth the risk."

Chances are very high that next season you and your team will be given numerous opportunities to win a big game, defeat a highly ranked opponent, or achieve something very special for your group. Wouldn't it be a shame if you were unprepared when that moment arrived? Make sure that doesn't happen. Be a champion. Turn your off-season into an investment season.

Optimize Your Performance

1. In groups, discuss how the stories of these teams above resonate with your team. Are we willing to put in the work to do everything right, knowing that there may not be a championship next season?

_____

_____

2. Answer these questions for yourself, write them down, and post them in your locker or someplace you will see them every day:

   a. What are my individual goals for next season?

_____

_____

_____

b. What specific things do I need to *start* doing/*stop* doing/*keep* doing on a daily, weekly, and monthly basis to give me the best opportunity to achieve these goals?

_____

_____

c. How will I record my progress?

_____

_____

_____

3.   Huddle up with your team and answer similar questions:

a. What are our team goals for next season?

_____

_____

b. What specific things do we need to *start* doing/*stop* doing/*keep* doing on a daily, weekly, and monthly basis to give us the best opportunity to achieve these goals?

_____

_____

c. How will we record our progress?

_____

_____

PART II: COMPETE

Winning the Competitive Game

Most people don't want to be part of the process. They just want to be part of the outcome. But the process is where you figure out who is worth being part of the outcome.

—Carey Lohrenz, first female F-14 fighter pilot

The entire sports world was stunned by the passing of Kobe Bryant and his daughter in a helicopter crash in January 2020. As people grappled with the legacy Kobe had left, the tributes started pouring in. One thing became abundantly clear: in the eyes of many, the 5-time NBA champion and 18-time All-Star was the ultimate competitor.

The stories about Kobe, his work ethic, and his "Mamba mentality" are legendary. He used to show up at 5 a.m. and practice for two hours . . . in high school. As an 18-year-old NBA rookie, one of his teammates watched him shooting by himself in the dark for two hours. When playing with Team USA, he often showed up and practiced for three hours before his first teammate arrived, and in one instance he spent six hours in the gym, refusing to leave until he made 800 shots.

Kobe Bryant watched everything he ate, and took care of his body to both prevent and recover from injuries. His mental preparation was a daily "workout of the mind," using mindful meditation that he claimed helped him to stay connected with his competitive drive. He was relentless about practicing the basics, doing the most basic footwork, dribbling, and shooting drills with and without the ball, with each hand, in his quest to win more championships. "Think of me as a person who has overachieved. That would mean a lot to me," said Bryant. "That means I put a lot of work in and squeezed every ounce of juice out of this orange that I could."

Bryant's competitive fire and astonishing work ethic set a standard that was not reachable for all of his teammates. It led to arguments, disagreements, and unrest in some of his teams. But for those of them who understood Kobe, they were inspired to be a better version of themselves. As George Mumford, the mindfulness coach who worked closely with both Michael Jordan's Bulls and Kobe's LA Lakers teams, told us, some of Kobe's teammates complained that he didn't pass the ball enough. "Yes, he does," said Mumford. "He passes it to those guys who are showing up and doing more work than everyone else, because they have earned his trust. Have you?" Great competitors not only drive themselves, but they inspire those around them.

Part II of this book is about competing. It is about pounding the rock, and encouraging, leading, and inspiring your teammates to do the same. It is about training yourself to respond to situations instead of reacting. It is about building the capacity to face your fears, embracing your mistakes, and getting comfortable with being uncomfortable. It will teach you how to focus on the process and daily grind, to "win the day," and to recognize the powerful tool your mind is on that journey to athletic success.

"Competing at the highest level is not about winning," said Joe Torre, the four-time World Series champion manager of the New York Yankees. "It's about preparation, courage, understanding, and nurturing your people and your heart. Winning is the result." So far you and your team have learned how to connect and build stronger relationships. This bond will allow you to compete, not just on game day but every single day. That is the way of a champion teammate. Read on and learn how.

9. Pound the Rock

If I am training on a holiday, most likely nobody else is—and that gives me the edge. If I'm supposed to run for 20 minutes and I get back and it's only 19:34, I'm going to jog in a circle for 26 more seconds. I'm never going to cut it short.

—Carli Lloyd, US Soccer

The San Antonio Spurs of the NBA had an extraordinary run of success from 1999–2017, winning at least 50 games per season and five NBA championships. They were famous not only for their consistency but for their work ethic, encapsulated by a quote, written in multiple languages on the walls of their training facility:

> When nothing seems to help, I go look at a stonecutter hammering away at his rock perhaps a hundred times without as much as a crack showing in it. Yet at the hundred and first blow it will split in two, and I know it was not that blow that did it, but all that had gone before. —Jacob Riis

There also is a statue of a stone and a hammer in the middle of the room, a constant reminder that the way to accomplish anything is to pound the rock, day after day, until it cracks. Practice after practice, day after day, season after season, the Spurs pound the rock. They get one percent better every day. They make practice the most challenging game of the week. They make mistakes, learn from them, and improve.

The San Antonio Spurs know that the first one hundred blows may not yield the outcome they hope for, but only through one hundred unsuccessful blows will come the one that cracks the rock, the one breakthrough victory, the next world title. Ask any Spurs player what it is all about to be a member of that team, and they will all tell you, "Pound the rock."

The greatest competitors in sports embrace the ethos of pound the rock and inspire others to do the same. They show up early. They stay late. They relentlessly work on the basics, mastering everything from footwork to simple techniques, done time and again until they become automatic. Gaining mastery is not a onetime thing—it's an everyday thing.

Hall of Fame basketball players such as Kobe Bryant and Michael Jordan were famous for their incredible work ethic and competitive drive. It drove some teammates crazy, but they eventually surrounded themselves with like-minded competitors. NFL Hall of Famer Peyton Manning was similarly competitive, not just on the practice field or in the weight room, but in the film room as well. No player was better prepared than he was come game day. Whether it is Sue Bird from the WNBA, Tiger Woods from the PGA, or former FIFA Player of the Year Carli Lloyd, name a famous athlete and we will show you an athlete that pounded the rock day after day.

Becoming a great teammate and building a group of high-impact competitors also requires the same type of effort. It is a process, not an event. It requires pounding the rock, day after day, blow after blow, until one day it all comes together, not because of a single event, but because of the hundred impactful moments that came before. First, you must model the relentless pursuit of excellence, because your teammates won't remember what you say, only what you do. Your work ethic will inspire others to do the same, and slowly but surely more teammates will get on board.

You may have heard people talking about the 10/80/10 rule in business and leadership. Every team has about 10 percent of people who do everything right. They are always early, stay late, and epitomize your core values. They are disciplined and seek to get better every day. They may not even be a starter on your team, and in fact oftentimes part-time players who are top 10 percenters are more motivating because they are willing to give everything and sometimes get no playing time in return.

Teams also have a bottom 10 percent, a group that is the opposite. They show little interest, they can be disruptive and hostile to teammates who are trying to buy in, and they don't care much about getting better or improving the group. They are the ones that drive coaches and leaders nuts, and while it is compelling to keep spending your time and energy on them, sometimes you have to use your time more wisely.

The rest of the team is the 80 percent. They are pretty reliable, do a decent but not spectacular job, and have some good days and some average ones. They will do what you ask of them but rarely more unless they are being watched, and while some may have some talent, they rarely reach their potential because the desire to improve and buy in just does not burn like it does in your top 10-percent people.

You can spend inordinate amounts of time and energy being distracted and frustrated by the bottom 10 percent. The secret of taking your team from good to great is getting as many of those 80 percenters into the top group. If you can take that top 10 percent, add some players, and take it to 20–30 percent, your team is going to be very good. If you can get more teammates buying in every single day, pounding the rock, taking extra reps, sleeping and eating well, and hitting the weight room, it soon becomes uncomfortable NOT to do these things. If you can engage your 80 percenters, pretty soon practice becomes more competitive and the standards are raised.

If you are a teammate that embraces the Pound the Rock mentality every single day, you are a leader, and you must go after the 80-percent teammates. When Tim Tebow was a Heisman Trophywinning quarterback at the University of Florida, he used to go into head coach Urban

Meyer's office every day and say, "Coach, let's go get some 80 percenters today."

On the teams John works with he always sits down with the leadership group preseason—these are the upper 10-percent team members—and identifies a few teammates in the 80-percent group whose ability and skill could most help our team get to the next level if we could engage them on a daily basis. Every single leadership group easily names a few teammates that could do this. Then, John assigns specific teammates to specific leaders and gives them accountability for bringing them into the top 10 percent that day. By giving leaders accountability and specific teammates to go after, it removes any ambiguity over who is responsible for elevating their teammate.

This process of identifying the 80 percenters works very well. One team John worked with identified a teammate with tremendous ability who was struggling to fit well with the group, which was detrimental to her focus and performance. The leaders knew she could become a huge difference maker for the team. They worked incredibly hard to bring her into the fold, understand what motivated her, and how they could help bring out her best performance every single day. Day after day the group persisted, and lo and behold a new, dominating teammate appeared. By season's end, the team was ranked in the Top 10 in the nation, and she was an NCAA Division I All-American!

If you are a top 10 teammate, you have tremendous influence. You are a leader, and your team needs you to engage with people one-on-one and inspire them to be better. People look up to you and want to be around you, so demand that if they are to hang with you, they must meet and exceed the team standards. Catch them being good when they step up, and reward the things you value. Once your 80-percent teammates recognize that they can be part of the inner circle, they will need less cajoling and motivation to step up. This season, identify and elevate your 80-percent teammates, and take your team from good to great.

Optimize Your Performance

1. Identify the Pound the Rock behaviors on your team. What do they look like? Show up early? Stay late? Play some wall ball? Perfect attendance in the weight room? Give out a ceremonial rock or hammer each week to the teammate that epitomizes Pound the Rock behaviors the most. The following week, the recipient gets to give it to another teammate. Write down your takeaways here.

    _____

    _____

2. In your leadership group, identify specific teammates in the 80-percent category that can make the biggest difference for the team this season. Assign specific individuals to each member of the leadership group and be accountable for your work with those teammates. Every week or two check in with the leadership group, and see how it is going, if you need to trade accountability partners, etc. Write down your takeaways here.

    _____

    _____

3. If you are part of a high school, college, or professional team, identify the new teammates/recruits and assign each of them to a member of the leadership group to start acclimatizing them into your culture. Teach them about Pound the Rock, for if you set the expectations and standards before they enter the building, they are more likely to meet them. Write down your takeaways here.

_____

_____

4. Find ways to reward people who move into the upper echelon of the team. Let them help select uniforms, menus on team meals, or playlists for the bus ride or pregame warm-up. People who get to weigh in are more likely to buy in! Write down your takeaways here.

_____

_____

10. Win the Day

The war is won before the battle begins.

—Sun-Tzu, *The Art of War*

The concept of Win the Day came to Jerry while working with the national championship men's tennis team at Middlebury College. Having lost in the finals the previous year, the guys were all excited to begin the journey again to win that championship. However, their approach was misguided.

Every teammate was talking about winning and beating and celebrating. The excitement was palpable yet became the cause for distraction and tension. *Having* to win will do that to an athlete. When Jerry felt the team's deep need to control the outcome of the season, he had them back off and suggested they talk about the little things they could do today at practice that would essentially be controlled and enable them to win the day. The phrase became their mantra every day, week, and month leading up to the NCAA Final Four. In the finals, they walked on the court wearing T-shirts that had Jerry's Way of Champions logo with the words WIN THE DAY on the back as a reminder of the task at hand. They were national champions in attitude, stature, and posture as they cruised to victory and were crowned champions.

Another favorite story that elucidates the Win the Day concept comes from Jerry's conversations with Steve Kerr, head coach of the Golden State Warriors. Jerry wanted to give to Steve a refreshing perspective that could help the athletes. One of the Warrior's core values is competitiveness. During the 2015 NBA Finals in Cleveland, the team was down two games to one. The media talked about a "must-win" game. Pressure and tension began to build on the players and staff. The team started to focus on outcomes and results instead of the things that they controlled.

Jerry and Coach Kerr had a phone call prior to game 4 where they discussed how to remedy this emotionally packed situation by focusing on things such as diving for the 50/50 ball, crashing the boards, boxing out, sprinting the lanes, playing "in-your-face" defense, and all the other little things that were controllable. Steve said that Jerry's idea was exactly what he needed to hear. He gave this advice to the team, and they rode the wave to winning the NBA championship. According to Steve, "They broke the code in game four." They were champion teammates together. They won the championship by winning the day, and by focusing on competing instead of trying to win.

The brilliant opening quote by the ancient Taoist warrior Sun-Tzu reminds us that you can accomplish victory by preparing well and having a strong commitment to competing prior to any game or contest. Being competitive for these purposes means focusing on executing all the controllable little things brilliantly, not the big things marginally. It's the difference between showing up to win vs. showing up to compete. When you show up to win the game, your focus is on outcomes and results, something you cannot control. Officials, weather, field conditions, and opponents all have a part to play in the outcome and are out of your control. This will cause you to get tight, tense, and tentative. When this happens, your confidence declines and self-doubt rises. Losing confidence results in a lackluster performance.

Conversely, when you show up to compete, your focus is on executing all the little things that you can control. This will allow you to feel calm, relaxed, focused, and stress-free. From this state of mind, you feel free, fluid, and your performance has the chance to be extraordinary.

When you do this, you may not win the game, but you are in a better position to do so. And this is what we call Win the Day.

NBA head coach Quin Snyder told us he calls the little things his "essential absolutes." Coach John Wooden claimed that he never talked about winning or beating an opponent. Teammates on his UCLA dynasty teams learned the lesson that competing like this gave them the chance to be their absolute best. The all-time winningest NCAA women's lacrosse coach, Cindy Timchal, told Jerry, "In our culture, the teammates never show up to win the game. We simply show up to compete." And compete they did on their way to seven consecutive national championships. Jerry was an intimate part of this dynasty, and he can tell you that every athlete on those teams became champion teammates by adapting and adopting the moniker Win the Day.

Optimize Your Performance

1. Reflect upon the story of Middlebury tennis. Does your team focus so much on winning that you forget to do the little things? What can you do to help yourself and others to win the day?

_____

_____

_____

2. What specifically can you *start* doing—that you are not currently doing—to win the day?

_____

_____

_____

3. What specifically can you *stop* doing—that you are currently doing—to win the day?

_____

_____

_____

4. Identify the top five controllable little things for your position and game that, when performed brilliantly, raises your level of play. When you gather these elements of success, what specific ways can you execute these in practice and gamelike conditions?

_____

_____

_____

5. Use this affirmation daily until you begin to see that change in your level of competing: *On this team, I compete like crazy with my hair on fire.*

6. Recite this affirmation often: *When I compete, I am difficult to beat.*

_____

_____

_____

11. Don't React. Respond!

The difference between responding and reacting is a choice. When you are reacting, they are in control. When you respond, you are. Learn.
—Henry Cloud, American author

John has had the honor of working with an amazing group of young women on the Colby College women's lacrosse team. Their coach, Karen Henning, is a brilliant coach who understands that there are advantages your team can gain from being mindful and building a strong culture, and John got to play a small role in helping that team come together. In 2017, they had an extraordinary season.

The team finished the regular season tied for first in the incredibly tough NESCAC conference, and won the NESCAC tournament for the first time since 2008. Along the way, they twice defeated Middlebury College, a multiple-time national champion, including in the NESCAC tournament semifinals on Middlebury's home field. The team was set to receive one of the top seeds for the NCAA tournament and looked forward to a few more home games. Then disaster struck.

There was a college baseball tournament and a youth gymnastics meet being held in Waterville, Maine, the same weekend as the NCAA tournament opening round. There were no hotel rooms. For that reason, NCAA denied Colby's bid to host, and the team lost the home field advantage they had earned through their high seeding.

There was anger, and sadness, and then disbelief, as the team was sent back on the road to Middlebury for a third matchup with an incredibly tough opponent. Colby could not have gotten a tougher opponent or place to play after a season of hard work. The team started to lose track of its narrative, and started to react and let outside forces control their fate. Those voices told the team how it got a raw deal. They told the team that life was unfair and it was impossible to go back and beat Middlebury again. The voices railed against the NCAA and the local hotels.

Colby women's lacrosse started reacting to things out of their control, instead of responding to the situation in front of them. They had stopped focusing on what could be controlled and had turned the focus to the uncontrollables. They were focused on all the reasons they should lose, instead of what they could do to compete and win. John knew they were in trouble and had to change the narrative. They had to write their own story. They had to stop reacting and start responding, or the game would be lost before it was even played.

Has this ever happened to your team? Has a bad call by an official, lousy weather, poor conditions, unruly fans or opponents ever gotten you off your game? Have you lost your head or changed your story because of these uncontrollable factors? It would be completely normal if it has. The difference between average teammates and great ones, the difference between average teams and championship teams, is that the best of the best do not react—they respond.

Author and leadership teacher Tim Kight has a wonderful equation that we love to share with teams we work with:

$$\textbf{Event (E)} + \textbf{Response (R)} = \textbf{Outcome (O)}$$

Every competition is filled with numerous events. There might be bad calls, funny bounces, and missed assignments. All of these events have an influence, but as Kight stresses, it is our response to those events that is a far greater determinant of the outcome than the events themselves. We do not control the events, but we do control our response.

Sadly, many athletes and coaches fail to respond. They react instead. And there are good reasons for this.

In the 1990s, Italian researchers stumbled upon a class of neurons in the brain that fire not only when an individual performs an action but also when that individual witnesses another person perform an action. They call this mirror processing. This is why you yawn when you see your teammate yawn in a team meeting, and you flinch when you see a teammate stub a toe or twist an ankle. Do you ever smile when you see someone smile? These reactions are governed by your mirror neurons, which allow you not only to simulate the actions of others but the emotions behind those actions as well. Researchers have used fMRI technology to test the effect of emotional attachment on brain function, and the results are extraordinary.

When you are playing a game, you are actually using a different region of your brain to judge a pass interference call or judge offside than you would in a neutral situation. The neutral decision-making areas of your brain actually disengage, and you use a part of your brain called your inferior parietal lobe. When you do this, your brain reacts as if *you* were the one performing the action. This is why sometimes your parents and coaches can completely lose it at the games they are highly invested in. Their brains react as if *they* were being fouled or having a goal unjustly called back.

This same mirror processing is also why teams feed off each other's energy, often either peaking and dominating together, or sulking and giving up at the same time. Team emotions are contagious, in both a positive and negative way. If our team tends to react to events, sometimes this will help us, such as when we score a big goal or make a great defensive play. We may have renewed energy, and play on the front foot, and this is great. But what if we lose our discipline? What if we fail to manage the scoreboard, the time clock, or possession? Reactions, at times, can be great, but they are also a crapshoot. And if the event is a negative one, they will hurt us.

On the other hand, a response is disciplined. It is trained. It is based upon our character, our morals, our life skills. It is controlled by us and our intentional actions. If there is a bad call, we play the next play instead of arguing the last play, because that is the only one we can affect. If we don't make the starting lineup, or play our favored position, we can react and get angry, whiny, and grumpy, or we can respond and focus on our effort, intensity, and play in a manner that ensures we get on the field the next game. We all know which of these choices will have a positive effect on our current and future performance. And we all know it is not by reacting. Great teammates don't react; they respond, and hold their teammates accountable for doing the same.

So what happened to Colby women's lacrosse in 2017? At practice that Tuesday, John asked the coaches to bring paper and pens to the locker room. They took the first fifteen minutes of practice and had each player write her own story. How does she want it to read? How does she want it to feel? What is your *why* for this weekend? They wanted to build their own story and let that be their narrative. John gave them the following prompt for their writing: "We are going back to Middlebury. We are the NESCAC champions, and now we have been given the privilege of competing for an NCAA championship. This is what is going to happen . . ."

And Colby lost, 10–9 on a last-minute goal. Life is not a fairy tale. Sometimes you compete your very best and you lose. That is the reality and the beauty of sports. But the moral of this story is this: Colby showed up and competed. They could have easily reacted to all that was unjust and gotten blown out. But they didn't. They played fantastic, disciplined lacrosse, and focused on the controllables. They fell agonizingly short. And after the game, they held their heads high and celebrated a fantastic season, a NESCAC championship, and a team bond that was stronger than ever.

Great teammates and championship teams don't react. They respond!

Optimize Your Performance

1. Reflect upon the story of Colby women's lacrosse shared above: Has there been a time when your team has reacted instead of responding and it has cost you a game? Have you lost a competition before it even started because you let others control the narrative? What could you have done differently in those moments?

_____

_____

2. Complete a team E + R = O exercise: Write down on a whiteboard all the events you react poorly to (bad calls, conditions, weather, playing time, positions, etc.). Break up into groups and have each group take one or two of these and write down how they react to these situations when they are not being disciplined, and how they could respond instead. Then, weave these into practices. Practice adversity. Practice responding, so when you see it in competition, you will already have experienced it. Write down your takeaways here.

_____

_____

3. Complete an individual E + R = O exercise: Break into pairs and share with your partner a time where you reacted badly to a situation. Discuss how you could have responded better and how that would have helped your performance and the team. Be prepared to share some of these with the team. Now, here is the important part: agree to hold each other accountable, and be willing to call out your teammate when they are reacting and not responding. Write down your takeaways here.

_____

_____

4. Bonus activity: Complete a personality assessment to gain more insight into how you react to certain situations. From DiSC to StrengthsFinder, there are many personality inventories you can use. John prefers to use E-Colors (www.equilibriainsports.com), because he has found it is a very powerful tool to help teammates understand each other and understand themselves. Write down your takeaways here.

_____

_____

12. Build the Capacity to Endure

Most people think that it is only going to get easier from here. Life is going to get easier. Basketball is going to get easier. School is going to get easier. It never gets easier. What happens is you become someone who handles hard stuff better. So make yourself a person that handles hard well, because if you have a meaningful pursuit in life, it will never be easy!

—Kara Lawson, Duke women's basketball coach

I have self-doubt. I have insecurity. I have a fear of failure. I have nights when I show up at the arena and I'm like, "My back hurts, my feet hurt, my knees hurt. I don't have it. I just want to chill." We all have self-doubt. You don't deny it, but you also don't capitulate to it. You embrace it.

—Kobe Bryant

Pressure is a constant in athletics. Whether it is a professional golfer like Justin Leonard standing over a putt to win the 1999 Ryder Cup for Team USA, to Michael Jordan hitting the game winner for the University of North Carolina in the 1982 NCAA finals, to Brandi Chastain about to take a penalty kick to win the 1999 World Cup, athletes from youth to the highest levels of sport face pressure. They feel stress. They face fear of letting down teammates and loved ones, just like you do. The difference between the best of the best that you watch on TV, and perhaps you or some of your teammates, is that they have built the capacity to embrace the pressure, stress, and fear. Have you?

One of the myths that lingers in the sporting world is that the top performers do not feel fear, stress, anxiety, worry, and doubt. They do, just like everyone reading this book does. They have just accepted that these things are the terms and conditions that they agree to when they play a sport, commit to a team, and chase something that matters to them.

The problem is that athletes often believe that something is wrong with them when they have natural worries and concerns. "Why am I feeling this, there must be something wrong," they often say to themselves. Then they are told by parents, coaches, books, etc., "You have to be more positive, more confident, more calm believe in yourself more, block out those thoughts, don't let them creep into your mind, you need to write a vision board, etc." Yet that is the worst thing you can do. Instead, you must accept them as natural and expected feelings and emotions. Or to put it more succinctly, in the words of performance psychologist Jonah Oliver:

"We worry about the things we care about. Welcome to being human!"

Oliver's clients include a who's who in professional golf, the Olympics and world championships, professional soccer and AFL, even the Porsche Le Mans world champion racing team. Combining his training in sport psychology and neuroscience, Oliver brings a simple and effective approach to facilitating peak performance. Some of his athletes are trying to hit winning putts in golf or score the winning goal in soccer, while others are putting their lives on the line in motorcycle racing or Le Mans.

They all face the same fears that you face, only on a bigger stage, but the feelings you encounter are no less valid or real. And as Oliver would tell you, your job is to focus on the right thing at the right time. You do this by developing your competency and accepting those feelings as the terms and conditions you signed up for to compete for your team.

The higher the level, the harder it gets—in school, sports, and life—and if you truly care about something meaningful in your life, it is going to be hard. It never gets easier, as Duke women's basketball coach Kara Lawson states above. Expert performers may make it look easy, but that is because they have developed great competence and ability through hard work!

Have you ever seen an interview where a star athlete comes off the field or court, and the first question the interviewer asks is, "You were looking really confident out there today, what was your secret?" Many coaches or parents have probably said to you, "Wow, you were playing with so much confidence today, well done!" But is that the case? Can we really see confidence? Can we read minds? Or, as Oliver says, "What looks like confidence or is called confidence is actually competence. Confidence is a feeling, competence is a behavior."

In order to develop our own competence that can withstand high-pressure moments, and to perform better in the moments when it counts, Oliver suggests three things:

1. **It's not about positive thinking, it's about taking positive action no matter what you fear or feel.** There are no gold medals handed out for the best positive self-talk. The medals are handed out for being able to perform no matter what the conditions, and you can only do that when you continuously focus on taking positive action, fully present in the moment. Be where your feet are. And as you prepare for an event, practice well, practice often, and develop competence so that you can perform your normal actions even under pressure. That is what will get you to the top.

2. **It's not about reducing pressure, it's about building the capacity to embrace more.** The secret is not in trying to forget the pressure, distract yourself, or ignore the moment.

Those things are counterproductive. The secret is to grow your ability to embrace pressure and stress, overcome perfectionist tendencies, deal with anger and disappointment, and retain full focus. In team sports, this means creating a team culture that promotes psychological safety and creates accountability that celebrates an athlete's willingness to take the potential winning shot or to ask for the ball when the game is on the line.

3. **It's not about motivation, it's about connecting to what matters.** The rah-rah speech makes for good Hollywood movies, but it's not what gets athletes to perform at the highest levels under pressure. Motivation must be intrinsic. Even the scariest situations seem less scary when they are important to us and align with our why. If you lose your why, your focus will turn to the stress and pain you are experiencing. This is how brains are hardwired, and the way to overcome it is purpose. When we align with our why, we can endure more than we think we are capable of.

In order to perform our very best under high stress and pressure, we must acknowledge fear, anxiety, and the other challenging feelings and emotions, not attempt to suppress them. When you do this, and understand why your brain acts this way—because you care—it will free up your prefrontal cortex to focus on executing your skills and the tactical plan, rather than spending all your time and energy in your head.

"Normalizing frees up so much of people's energy trying to control their internal psychological state vs. realizing that it's the price of entry, that it's ok," concludes Oliver. "All you need to do is make room for it, embrace it, bring yourself back into the present in order to focus on the task at hand and get after it!"

So go ahead, give it a shot. Let's be great at practice so that, day by day, we are developing our competence and embracing any fear, stress, and anxiety as the welcome price of admission for signing up to play a sport. Treat it like a muscle group in the weight room. You cannot ignore or distract your way to a new personal best in the deadlift. You show up, do the work, and build capacity and strength over time.

When your moment comes, know that you have the love and support of your teammates, your coaches, and your family and friends, who respect you for having the courage to be in the arena with the game on the line. Then just do what you have already done thousands of times before. Make game day a normal competition, albeit on a special day. Don't make it more than that.

Optimize Your Performance

1. In your group, discuss the terms and conditions you all agreed to by becoming part of this team. Do they include competition for spots on the team or travel roster? Is practice supposed to be competitive? Do you have to battle for playing time every day? Discuss ways you can accept these terms and use them to make the team better, not stress the team out.

_____

_____

2. Make practices competitive: If your only competitive days are game day, you have already lost. Coach Anson Dorrance and the University of North Carolina women's soccer program have won 22 NCAA titles, and if you ask any player, they will tell you that game days are the easy ones. The US women's soccer team constantly speaks about the hardest games being intrasquad scrimmages. Always play for something, keep score, and make sure the result has consequences.

_____

_____

3. Replicate stressful moments as closely as possible: Shooting a one-and-one free throw to tie a game with one second left, the crowd screaming in your face, and your heart thumping through your chest is very different then laughing with your friends, chucking balls at the basket at the beginning of practice. So do 10 burpees and then make the free throw. End your line sprint drills by a player having to make a free throw at the point of exhaustion.

———————————————————————————————————

———————————————————————————————————

4. Embrace mistakes in your culture: The more your teammates feel psychologically safe, respected, and accepted, the more likely they will build the capacity to handle pressure situations. If your teammates fear making mistakes, because they are punished by coaches or ridiculed by teammates, that is what will be on their mind when the spotlight is on them in high-pressure moments. Pick up your teammates after every mistake, and their fear will diminish.

———————————————————————————————————

———————————————————————————————————

13. Get Comfortable Being Uncomfortable

Comfort the challenged and challenge the comfortable.
—Ric Charlesworth, Australian Olympian

Christian Pulisic showed an uncanny ability with the soccer ball from a very young age. His parents, Mark and Kelly, were excellent players in their own right, and Mark was a professional soccer coach when Christian was a child. Christian often played up a year or two, dribbling around players a head taller and demonstrating a flair and creative streak not often seen in young American kids.

At age 12 he was selected to the US Under-14 National pool, and he continued to blossom as he played with the PA Classics in Pennsylvania. Although his parents continued to say no to great opportunities, protecting Christian's love of other sports and his childhood, by the time he reached his midteens he had a choice. Would he stay comfortable, or would he take the leap to uncomfortable and propel his abilities and career to a new level? He chose to be uncomfortable.

Pulisic's rise through the youth ranks was crystalized on December 13, 2013—a date that changed his life and is now tattooed on his arm—when he led the US U-17 national team to a 4–1 victory over mighty Brazil. The phones started ringing with offers to move overseas, at an age no young American had done before. "He wasn't ready at first," his father told John on our *Way of Champions Podcast*, "but about six months later he came to Kelly and I and said, 'I'm ready, let's go.'"

Pulisic and his father moved to Dortmund, Germany, just prior to his 16th birthday, with Mark taking a coaching position at Borussia Dortmund and Christian joining their youth teams. He left his friends, familiar food, and a familiar language to stretch himself as a player and a person. "It was the hardest thing I have ever done in my life," wrote Pulisic in his recent book *Pulisic: My Journey So Far*.

Knowing he would endure injuries, hardships, and great difficulty along the way, Mark and Christian moved into an apartment, cleared off one of the walls, and wrote two words: NO EXCUSES.

"It was a difficult time," his father told us. "It was his dream, it was led by him, and I told him when it was no longer his dream, we could go home. But as long as he held this dream, no excuses." And there were plenty of opportunities for excuses.

For the first few months of 2014, Pulisic did not have his European Union passport, so he could practice but not play. He sat through hours of school in a language he did not understand, and often thought to himself, "What am I doing here? Is this really what I want?" But Pulisic persisted, and at age 17 he made both his Dortmund and US men's national team debuts.

He eventually was sold to Chelsea FC of the English Premier League for $73 million, and has become the face of American soccer. Yet along the way he has encountered numerous injuries, coaching changes, lack of playing time, and even depression, to go along with famous goals and winning the 2021 UEFA Champions League. As his father describes it, "It's definitely not for everyone."

We live in a world where it can seem that greatness is handed to a chosen few, who seemingly stroll through life making millions of dollars, sinking three-pointers with ease, winning gold medals, and making the sports they play look easy. But behind the scenes, every single one of those stars you watch on television has one thing in common: they have gotten comfortable being uncomfortable.

They have grinded and practiced many long, lonely hours. They have endured frustration, injury, numerous setbacks, and disappointment. Those moments we watch them on TV are but a fraction of the unseen hours they have spent with no one watching, in pain, in tears, and asking themselves, "Is this all worth it?" Kobe Bryant may have been famous for his insatiable "Mamba mentality," but everyone at the top has some level of that drive.

Do you? Does your team?

Everyone wants to win the game when the first whistle blows. Everyone might have wanted to win the night before. But what about six months prior? A year prior? At 6 a.m. in the weight room months before your next game?

The weight room is a good analogy, because if you have ever been in one, you know that those last few reps are the most uncomfortable, and the ones that count the most. Pushing for one extra rep when it really hurts, and doing that one extra sprint when it would be easier to push it off until tomorrow, are the moments that add up to excellence. Time and again you will be presented with a choice: comfort or discomfort. The more times you choose discomfort, the faster you will improve. The more times you choose comfort, the more you stay the same.

Your goal should be to build a team that chooses discomfort and stretch, over taking the easy way out. Everyone has a bad day when they are not at their best physically or mentally, and that is when you need teammates and team standards that don't let you slip.

One of our favorite quotes is from former US President Calvin Coolidge: "Nothing in this world can take the place of persistence. Talent will not; nothing is more common than unsuccessful men with talent." He is correct. The world is full of people who have ample ability yet lack the willingness to suffer for a greater cause. It is up to you, as a part of your team, to make sure that is not a phrase that describes your team at the end of this season. Don't be an unsuccessful team with talent.

Most athletes and teams will not ever achieve their true potential, because the thought of suffering and discomfort frightens them. Some people just do not like being out of their comfort zone. Others have a fixed mindset and never try hard because they are afraid that if they give their best and come up short, they are some kind of failure (which of course they are not).

It is easy to coast through a drill, or a play or two, because you do not notice the detrimental effect in the short term. If you don't hustle back on defense and nothing comes of it, or cut that wind sprint a few inches short of the line, no one will notice, right? But we do notice, on the scoreboard, months later. When given the choice of whether to embrace suffering or to pull back, some athletes often choose the easy path. That is why they will not make it. And that is why you must choose discomfort.

Anson Dorrance from the University of North Carolina women's soccer program once encountered Mia Hamm, the reigning college player of the year and already one of the top players in the world, training by herself early one morning on a hot, humid summer day. As he watched, she pushed herself through sprint after sprint, falling to the ground and gasping for breath after each. He wrote the following message to her:

"The true vision of a champion is someone bent over, drenched in sweat, at the point of exhaustion, when no one else is watching."

Mia Hamm went on to become the best player in the world, not only because she had talent and great coaching, but because she was willing to suffer more than her competitors. Is your team willing to suffer? Are you willing to be uncomfortable and an example to your teammates of how to exist day after day on the edge of your comfort zone?

If not, you can still do a lot of things in life, but becoming an elite athlete, or a championship team, is probably not one of them.

There are things that are more important than ability. Choosing discomfort is the path to the top. Being uncomfortable is the elite team's best friend!

Optimize Your Performance

1. As a group, reflect on the stories above about Christian Pulisic and Mia Hamm. What do we need to *start* doing to be more comfortable in a state of discomfort? What do we need to *stop* doing? What do we need to *keep* doing so that, day after day, we are pushing the envelope and improving?

   _____

   _____

   _____

2. The Anti-Talent Show: Kudos to our friend Trevor Ragan from The Learner Lab (www.TheLearnerLab.com) for this one. Everyone on the team, coaches included, pick a skill you cannot do. You now have two weeks to learn it and demonstrate it in front of the team. Maybe it is singing, playing an instrument, juggling, a new card trick, etc. Learning new things and having to demonstrate them publicly is a great way to get uncomfortable.

3. The Clemson Football "Safe Seat": Coach Dabo Swinney and Clemson football have had a great run of recent success, and one of the reasons they have is due to their team culture. The "safe seat" is a big part of it. They place a chair in the middle of the locker room and each player is asked to sit in it and answer questions about their life. It is "safe" because whatever is said never leaves the room. Getting in front of your peers and being vulnerable, telling your story to the group, can be incredibly uncomfortable, and incredibly powerful.

4. Get your reps: The best way to get comfortable with discomfort is to put yourself in uncomfortable situations often. It means competing hard in practice, doing extra work when no one is watching, speaking publicly, answering questions in class, practicing challenging conversations, or participating in any other situation that is difficult. The more you do it, the more confident and comfortable you will be.

14. Develop Great Habits, Break the Bad Ones

Results are a lagging measure of our habits. We get what we repeat.
—James Clear, author of *Atomic Habits*

NFL Hall of Famer Jerry Rice is known for many things. He was a three-time Super Bowl champion, and upon his retirement in 2005, after 20 years in the league, he held the all-time records for catches, receiving yards, touchdowns, most 1,000-yard receiving seasons, and most net combined yards. He played in eight conference championship games and four Super Bowls, and for eleven consecutive seasons he was named an NFL All-Pro. Jerry Rice was a superstar among superstars.

What is less known about Rice were all the things he did to reach this level. He was drafted out of a small college called Mississippi Valley State, and even though he was a first-round pick, he continually sought to build the type of habits that would persistently elevate his game. For 20 years he showed up early and stayed after practices. He was famous for his grueling six-day-per-week off-season workouts, which teammates would join from time to time but drop out of quickly.

Jerry Rice was never the fastest receiver, so he made up for it by maximizing his precise route running, quick change of direction and reaction time, and great leaping ability. He was also famous for his incredible endurance, built by daily five-mile runs and hill intervals, run by a player whose position demanded more speed than endurance. When the fourth quarter of games came around, Rice excelled. As he often stated, "Today I will do what others won't so tomorrow I can do what others can't."

There is one Jerry Rice habit that really stands out and is worth discussing. When you watch the vast majority of receiving drills in a football practice, a receiver runs the route, catches the pass, and sprints a few steps before turning and slowly jogging back to the line. But not Jerry Rice. As his former teammate Bo Eason told us on the *Way of Champions Podcast*, the first time he witnessed Jerry Rice practice, he was blown away. While others jogged back to the line, Rice caught the ball and, wherever he was on the field, he SPRINTED into the end zone. Every. Single. Time. As Eason watched Rice do this over and over, he finally asked him why he was doing that. "Every time these hands touch that ball," Rice told him, "that ball goes in the end zone. Just like it's supposed to in the game. Why would I practice any differently?"

Habits are the building blocks of your success, and recent research estimates that approximately 45 percent of our daily actions are habitual, meaning they are done while we are performing and thinking about other things. We think many if not all of our actions, from how we exercise to what we eat, are forces of will, but nearly half of the things we do every day are repeated in the same context often enough to become habits. The question you must ask yourself is the following: "Are my daily habits taking me closer to my desired future?" For as author James Clear says, "Results are a lagging measure of your habits. We get what we repeat."

Clear's book *Atomic Habits* has been translated into more than 50 languages and has sold over 10 million copies for a reason. People know how powerful habits are, and they want to build good ones and break their less helpful ones. Clear provides you with a pathway to do so, and it is worth exploring some of his main ideas. Here are three of them:

1. "Results are a lagging measure of your habits. You get what you repeat."

Eating a salad for lunch vs. eating a burger and fries is no big deal in the short term. You do not notice it in the moment or on the day, but over time you realize how much your bad habits cost you and your good habits earn you. It is the same in sports. If you choose not to work hard or focus today, it's not that big a deal in the short run, but compounded over time the bad days add up, and those athletes who link together good days will surpass you.

Our society is very outcome driven, especially on social media, where we share our highlights but never our struggles. We are inundated with results all the time, and we overvalue the results, while we tend to undervalue the process. Winners and losers often have the same goals, yet have very different outcomes. In other words, says Clear, goals are necessary but not sufficient. Achieving a goal only changes your life for a moment, but if you don't change the bad habits, eventually you will be right back where you started.

2. "Habits matter for both external and internal results."

The visible results of both good and poor habits are evident, but those external items are only half the battle. Internally, every action you take is a vote for the type of person you want to be, says Clear. The votes add up over time, and you gain evidence about the type of person you are becoming. This does not simply alter your results; it changes your identity. Proper habits give you more belief in the person you are becoming, and causes you to not just resist the bad things but to say, "I am the type of person who exercises every day/ eats well/sleeps well/is a great teammate."

3. "We do not rise to the level of our goals; we fall to the level of our systems."

Successful people are outcome aware but purpose and process driven, and nothing drives the process better than great systems. Very often, says Clear, we think we need to change our outcomes, but what really needs to change are the habits (how you build the system) and the system (the process of achieving those results.) Another word for systems could be culture, which Clear calls "the shared habits of the group." When we all value the same positive habits and behaviors, then we live and work in an environment where it is easier to make the right choices and ignore the wrong ones. Or in other words, bad habits repeat themselves not because we want them to happen, but because we have a bad system around them. Create systems that reinforce the good!

With these ideas in mind, think about yourself and your role on this team. What habits do you have that are bringing you closer to your personal goals and our shared goals? How are they helping bring us together? Or is the opposite happening? Are your/our "less than good" days compounding and taking you/us further away from our goals? Does our group need to build some better habits so that it is easier to progress than digress? We imagine the answer to all these questions is yes. So what shall we do?

We suggest you follow what Clear calls the "Four Laws of Behavior Change." Habits have four parts:

- Cue: something that triggers a behavior. If we want to develop a good habit, make your cues obvious so they will prompt you to act. Chop the fruit or veggies ahead of time and put them in the front and center of the fridge so you grab them instead of a high sugar bar. Put your running shoes next to your bed and wear your gear so you can hop out of bed and run instead of finding excuses not to.

- Craving: something that makes a desired behavior more attractive. This is where team culture comes in. It is easier to do the right thing when everyone else is doing the right thing. A parent might reinforce behavior by saying, "You get to play video games for every minute you exercise/practice/do chores." In a team setting, the social environment really matters, and good culture makes it uncomfortable NOT to do the desired behaviors.

- Response: make it easy and as convenient as possible to do the things you want to do and to avoid the things you don't. Eating too much ice cream? Don't put it front and center in your freezer. Duct tape the ice cream shut and shove it way back under other stuff. When you reduce the friction to good choices, you are more likely to make better choices. In other words, design a system that makes the good behavior convenient.

- Reward: make it satisfying to do something right. This does not mean effusive or false praise from a parent or coach, but it does mean catch someone being good. Clear calls this the "Cardinal Rule of Behavior Change": "Behaviors that are immediately rewarded get repeated. Behaviors that are immediately punished get avoided." We are not advocating physical punishment here as much as we are advocating coaches and parents being very intentional to catch people being good and to highlight the right behaviors.

If you want to break a bad habit, simply do the opposite. Reduce exposure to the cues that set you off on the wrong path, and make it unattractive to behave that way. Make it hard to complete the bad habits, and make it unsatisfying if you do. Don't leave the video game equipment out on the table. Better yet, don't buy it in the first place and save yourself from all those agonizing decisions every night.

Finally, Clear suggests that every few months we reflect and review. Celebrate your wins by asking yourself, "What went well?" Acknowledge your losses by asking, "What needs work still?" And come up with your next plan by asking, "Where do I go from here?" Then do it all over again.

Your team's results this season will be a lagging measure of the habits you build and repeat three, six, twelve months and more before you even start. Just like Jerry Rice, you need to build great habits, so that even on the days you feel less motivated, your habits carry you through and leave a net positive. Good luck.

Optimize Your Performance

1. Reflect on the story about Jerry Rice running into the endzone every time he touches the ball. What are some habits you could build that would turbocharge your development as individuals and as a team? As a team, share these answers and come up with 1–2 habits that are the most beneficial that we need to *start* doing, and 1–2 that are the most detrimental that we need to *stop* doing. Write it down, post it on the wall, and have everyone sign and commit to being an agent for change.

---

2. Do a team book read of *Atomic Habits* by James Clear. John has done this with a few of the collegiate teams that he advises, and it has been very beneficial in clarifying the small things that have huge impacts on performance. It will help you create new systems and a new identity around small, process-oriented steps toward excellence.

3. Write down your answer to the following two questions, and be prepared to share within groups and with the team.

    a. What is one habit that we have that is so essential we need to keep it no matter what?

    _____

    _____

    b. What is one habit we have that we would like to break right away?

    _____

    _____

15. Embrace the Setbacks

You lose yet in this way you gain.

—Lao-Tzu, *Tao Te Ching*

Lindsey Jacobellis is one of the greatest snowboarders in history: a five-time world champion, ten-time X Games gold medalist, and a five-time Olympian in the sport of snowboardcross. She started off as a skier but switched to snowboarding when she was eight years old and her house burned down, destroying all of her skiing equipment. She quickly rose through the ranks, and in 2006 at the Turin Olympics was poised to win the gold medal as she carried a three-second lead into the final jump of the race.

Attempting to fire up the crowd on the jump, Jacobellis threw a huge method air and crashed, and before she could slide across the finish line she was passed by Tanja Frieden and finished second. Defeat was snatched from the hands of victory, and her crash was beamed across the globe. For the next 15 years, she dominated X Games and world championship events, but injuries and crashes kept derailing her Olympic gold dreams. Every time the Olympics rolled around, replays of her 2006 crash, and questions about her failure to win gold, would enter the national spotlight. It seemed her career would be defined by one fateful mistake in 2006, and she would be better known for one blooper instead of a lifetime of achievement.

But Jacobellis was not to be deterred. She hired a mental skills

Optimize Your Performance

1. Reflect upon the story of Lindsey Jacobellis, or another story of disappointment and failure that is more personally relevant, and ask the following questions:

   a. What do you need to *start* doing—that you are not currently doing—to embrace setbacks and failure and become a better teammate to others?

   _____

   _____

   b. What do you need to *stop* doing—that you are currently doing—to embrace failure and setback and become a better teammate to others?

   _____

   _____

   _____

c. What do you need to *keep* doing when it comes to dealing with setbacks that will make you a better teammate?

_____

_____

_____

2. Use failure and mistakes to your advantage by implementing these ideas:

a. Remember that it is entirely impossible for any of us to always be successful, competent, and achieving. Failure is the rent we pay to occupy the apartment of athletics. Performance is a roller coaster and to think otherwise is a mistake itself. Be a mindful teammate by explaining this to others on the team.

b. True failure and setback can be defined as our unwillingness to see the positive perspective, take fearless risks, grow and improve from them, and find out how good you and your teammates really are.

c. You are never as great as your biggest victory nor as bad as your worst failure. Refuse to let outcomes such as loss and setback determine your worth or that of your team.

16. First Fly in a Chair

If your mind is empty, it is always ready for anything; it is open to everything.
In the beginner's mind there are many possibilities; in the
expert's mind there are few.
—Shunryū Suzuki, author of *Zen Mind, Beginner's Mind*

Many of the best athletes in the world embrace mindfulness and most have a meditation or visualization practice that they have built to optimize performance. This has been happening behind the scenes for many years. Even Michael Jordan, following his winning shot against the Utah Jazz in 1997 for one of his NBA championships, ran over to the bench and loudly commented to his teammates about his visualization practice, "This stuff really works!"

Ryan Bernacchi, a retired US Navy captain, Top Gun instructor, and former commander of the world-acclaimed performance flight acrobatic team the Blue Angels, knows something about mindfulness, meditation, and visualization. Ryan recently was a guest on our *Way of Champions Podcast*, where he talked extensively about teamwork and culture. One of the essential tools for his teams that he shared was how he and his entire team would simulate every flight using the ancient skill of mindful meditation visualization. He called it "flying in a chair."

The night before a mission or a Blue Angels air show, he would sit in a chair and close his eyes and imagine the entire flight ahead. He would make all the calls as lead pilot, out loud, and visualize every takeoff, maneuver, and landing. He would then repeat it over and over until he had seen and felt the entire mission before he did it in real time. He mentioned how all great pilots fly every flight in their heads before flying the actual mission by emptying their minds of the daily chatter then filling them with the mission at hand. It was in this quiet time that his confidence was gained and his inner voice said, "I'm ready!" This is how his squadron became trustful, connected, and caring teammates. You can as well.

Similarly, Coach Phil Jackson was the master of using mindful meditation with the Chicago Bulls and Los Angeles Lakers on his way to winning eleven championship rings. In Jackson's book *Eleven Rings*, he devotes several detailed pages on his thoughts about and use of the *Zen Mind, Beginners Mind* approach to his team's performance. To help players on both teams become better teammates, quiet the chatter of their minds, and focus on the nature of the inner game, he introduced the athletes to the concept of mindfulness.

Simply defined, mindfulness means to be aware and pay attention to the present moment with intention. It's about focusing on what is happening right now. Phil would get the players to sit in a room for ten or so minutes. He called it "the warrior room." He wasn't trying to make them into Buddhist monks; it was to help them become more connected and focused teammates.

All the athletes who took part in this voluntary exercise loved it. It was a special, unified group who were, in the words of Vietnamese teacher Thich Nhat Hanh, "dwelling happily in the present moment," with quiet, simple, and clear minds. Phil Jackson found through such practice that when his athletes marinate themselves fully in the inner game, they develop a deeper, stronger awareness of each other, and they fully focus on the present moment of the basketball game and being a great teammate.

One of Jackson's protégés, Golden State Warriors head coach Steve Kerr, knows something about championships as well and has chosen mindfulness as one of the team's core values. In conversations with Steve, we have talked about the importance of mindful meditation and visualization to help him with his leadership and to help his team be great teammates. We tell you all this in hopes that you will consider visualization and meditation as a skill to learn and use as you become the best teammate you can be.

There is an ancient Taoist proverb that states, "If you know the art of breathing you have the strength of ten tigers." Over the years Jerry has trained thousands of coaches and athletes to have tiger strength using a 2,500-year-old form of Buddhist meditation called Vipassana, a Pali word that when translated means "insight." This inner game of visualization meditation practice relies on the awareness that breathing is happening and using the breath as a focal point to quiet what Buddhists call the "monkey mind."

This meditative state of mind, this "still point," is a sacred space that raises awareness and makes movement effortless and confidence more robust. It helps us to find balance and keep it in our lives. It is a source of positive energy and helps us to remain connected with our teammates in a positive way. It has a direct, powerful influence on you and your team's performance.

As the thirteenth-century Japanese Buddhist teacher Nichiren states, "If the spirit of many in body but one in mind prevails among the people, they will achieve all their goals, whereas if one in body but different in mind, they achieve nothing remarkable."

It is interesting to notice how animals instinctively know and use a method of stillness in nature. They all meditate. Observe the heron poised motionless on one leg, the monkey climbing to the uppermost branch, the snake basking in the warmth of the summer sun, or the cat lying on a pillow, eyes focused on a small object. Such stillness prepares the inner environment for a deep, peaceful meditative state.

Being mindful will help you win the inner game and become a champion teammate. It will help you to see clearly and act more appropriately when it comes to being the best teammate you can be. Mindfulness has actually become profoundly relevant in mainstream America, being embraced by hospitals helping patients to heal, military groups wanting to focus, educational systems hoping to facilitate learning, musicians wishing to be more present, actors trying to stay in the moment, and countless elite athletes working to maximize their performance.

You can become a better teammate when you practice mindfulness using meditation and visualization. Meditation is a learned strategy that can strengthen your wishes to become more inspired, self-aware, and a better leader on your team. There is not a better venue for practicing meditation than athletics. The benefits are realized almost immediately.

So, don't forget to take your "meds" . . . meditations, that is.

Optimize Your Performance

1. With your team, discuss how Top Gun instructor and commander of the Blue Angels Ryan Bernacchi's story has helped you understand how visualization can help you perform better. How about the story of the Chicago Bulls and LA Lakers? Are you ready to incorporate some mindfulness and visualization into your regular team activities? Discuss as a group.

   _____

   _____

   _____

2. If you're ready, begin this inner game with eyes closed, in a quiet place, free from interference, and sit comfortably in a chair with your back straight and feet on the floor. Drop your arms into your lap, and take the following steps:

   a. Begin by taking three deep, controlled breaths, holding the oxygen in your lungs for three seconds before you exhale. Notice how this procedure has an instant effect on your body and mind, relaxing you immediately. Then, stop and return to normal breathing.

   b. Simply notice that breathing is happening. Watch it come in and go out. Do not control its natural flow other than to have it go through the nostrils.

c. When your mind wanders—and it will—simply acknowledge it and direct it back by saying, "Wandering, come back." Don't be concerned about wandering, because it's natural. In fact, the act of being aware of the wandering and bringing your attention back to the breath actually helps you to develop strong attention skills when you are competing in everyday life. It develops what we call "meta-attention." Wandering is an integral aspect to the full meditation practice.

d. Do this "breath watching" for about five to eight minutes, then switch gears and begin to visualize by *feeling* yourself being how you wish to be as the champion mindful teammate bringing out the best in others. Visualize for about four minutes.

e. Following your visualization, recite a few short, positive affirmations that nurture and support your visualizations. Unlike visualizations which involve how you feel and what you see, these strong statements influence what you say and, more importantly, how you think. Thoughts strengthen or weaken you and determine the direction in which you go. Affirmations are spiritual gems that keep you on the path to lead your teammates with heart. Write them out on index cards, and as you recite them, feel the words as if they are real and happening now.

3. What specifically can you do to make sure you incorporate the visualization process as a routine into your daily life?

_____

_____

_____

4. How can you specifically help other teammates to adopt and adapt the mindfulness approach to their athletic and leadership preparation? As science has shown, overall performance in sports, and leadership as a teammate, would be greatly enhanced by doing what other champion teams have done to raise their levels.

_____

_____

_____

17. Silence Stinking Thinking

We choose to have positive thoughts. Nothing can depress or upset our power-ful and positive life force . . . not mood swings, not even negative circumstances affect this rock. We refuse to whine or cause drama.

—Anson Dorrance,
22-time national champion head coach,
North Carolina women's soccer

We all have highly impactful moments in our lives, where a coach, teammate, or teacher says something that sticks with us forever. Jerry often tells the story of how one college professor's comment, just a few positive words, has impacted the trajectory of his life to this day. The teacher was handing back a 10-page paper to all the students in this writing class, with grades in red at the top. Not being a stellar student at the time, Jerry was shocked and pleased to see that he had received an A+ for his work. He thought this was a mistake, but as the teacher handed it to Jerry, he quipped, "Lynch, you can really write well." Jerry ran with that comment, held it close to his heart, and as of this writing has published 17 books. His thoughts since that moment long ago have been that he IS a good writer.

John had a similar experience in high school, only his teacher handed back a paper with a big, fat red "F" on it. "No way I deserve an F on this paper," said John to his teacher. "I know it's better than most papers in this class." His teacher looked at him and said, "I am not giving you a grade based upon what others can do. I am giving you a grade based upon what you can do, and this is poor." He then proceeded to throw John's books out the third-story classroom window and kicked him out of class. And as John left, his teacher yelled out, "You are a great writer! Act like it." John has dedicated all of his books to this teacher for this life-changing gift.

Both John and Jerry were lucky enough to have mentors that filled their minds with belief. There's a legendary Cherokee story that is emblematic of the greatest battles we ever fight, the one between our good and bad thoughts. An old Cherokee grandpa says to his grandson, "A fight is inside me. It's between two wolves. One is evil and has thoughts of anger, hate, greed, envy, and resentment. The other wolf is good and has thoughts of joy, love, peace, truth, compassion, and kindness." The grandson thought about it for a minute then asked his grandpa, "Which one will win?" The reply was simple: "The one who wins is the one you feed." As a champion teammate, you get opportunities every day to feed the wolf that will fill your own head, and our teammates' heads, with positive, life-changing thoughts.

One of the most important concepts we teach is "feelings equal function," elaborated on in "Be an Elevator" in Part I. Each day we have over 70,000 thoughts. We become defined by these thoughts. Choosing negative thoughts each day leads to negative feelings, and science has proven to us that feelings greatly affect how we perform and behave. Changing your thoughts will create a new road map to a new and higher functioning future.

We are all shaped by our minds. We become the teammate that we are by what we think. We love, lead, and compete as we think, and no one other than ourselves can alter our minds. We control our thoughts and our thoughts then control us. It takes work to emancipate our minds from this "stinking thinking," and this is what we hope to help you with in this book.

Start by thinking about how you may feed the bad wolf: I'm not good enough; I'm not smart enough; I'm not big or strong enough; I'm not fast enough; I'll never be able to do that; I'm a failure; I'm not a good leader . . . and on and on. When you replace these thoughts with positive ones, your life changes. It is palpable. Try it. Say, "I can do it, I am strong, I am fast, I am good enough," and repeat these phrases often. In the words of Hall of Fame baseball athlete Wade Boggs, "A positive attitude causes a chain reaction of positive thoughts, events, and outcomes which sparks extraordinary results."

As a champion teammate, tell your teammates that their thoughts will strengthen or weaken them. They have a power of their own. Steph Curry of the Golden State Warriors reminds us that the body feeds off the mind. When your thoughts are positive, you relax and become calm, and thereby your performance is enhanced. Tell your teammates that science has proven that thoughts are intricately intertwined with our physical selves, and that is good news for higher levels of competitiveness as well.

Remember this: the direction your thoughts go is the direction your body will follow. Do your part through words and actions to elevate your teammates' thoughts about themselves and the group. This does not mean you are dishonest or accept behaviors that fall below the standards of your team. It means to pick and choose your moments and recognize the influence and impact those words and deeds have.

Positivity can change your life, enhancing your ability to be a high-impact teammate. One small positive comment at the right time can light up a teammate's life. A negative comment can cast them into darkness. You can be the light that has a high impact in your culture and life. Thoughts change lives. As an exceptional teammate, make it part of your work to hand out good thoughts to all whom you love.

Optimize Your Performance

1. The first exercise that can help you to impact your teammate using positive thoughts would be to return to Part I, "Be an Elevator," and use the RIVER Effect as a way to encourage, empower, and make your teammates feel important and valued.

2. What do you need to *start* doing—that you are not currently doing—to create positive thinking habits?

    _____

    _____

3. What can you *stop* doing—that you are currently doing—to create positive thought habits?

    _____

    _____

    _____

4. What do you need to *keep* doing—that you are currently doing—
to keep your mind focused on positive, performance-enhancing
thoughts?

_____

_____

_____

5. Look for ways to catch one of your teammates doing something
right and commend them on such. In sports, the whistle is a device
to catch athletes doing something wrong so that it will be corrected.
Rarely do they get caught doing what's right, and the impact when
that is done is massive.

6. Create positive self-directing affirmations that can be given to a
teammate or used by you on a consistent basis. Here are a few to get
you started: When I compete, I am difficult to beat. All my failures
and mistakes are wonderful opportunities to learn and improve.
I refuse to let my fears interfere with my potential. I am a tough,
fearless, and strong impact leader. My influence is never neutral, and
my aim is to light up my team. I commit to never give up.

7. Discuss with your team how the Cherokee story about the two wolves impacts your team? Which wolf do we feed when the pressure builds?

_____

_____

_____

PART III: LEAD

Winning the Leadership Game

Leadership is a matter of how to be, not how to do.
—Frances Hesselbein, former CEO, Girl Scouts of America

There is a need to have good leaders. Incompetent leaders compromise the strength of the group, allowing lesser groups to take charge and win. Take time to establish great leadership.
—Sun-Tzu, *The Art of War*

In today's volatile and uncertain world of sports we need to have good leaders if we are to have great teams. Yet often we simply tell our people to be better leaders rather than teaching them to lead. Many years ago, Phil Jackson, then coach of the Los Angeles Lakers of the NBA, asked Jerry to send a copy of his book *The Way of the Champion* to a struggling and ineffective athlete he was coaching at the time. His name was Kobe Bryant.

The Lakers were underperforming as a unit. While Kobe was personally being successful, his teammates were not. Phil wanted to harness Kobe's competitive drive and use it in a positive way to lead his teammates and inspire them to be better. He thought that the section in the book on conscious leadership would help direct Kobe into being a better teammate and leader by focusing on making his teammates better, by distributing the ball, encouraging others, and showing them more compassion. Kobe read the book, adopted the changes, and became a better teammate. The Lakers performance improved drastically, and they were happier with their "new" teammate leader. Later on, in an interview with the *Orange County Register,* Kobe mentioned how much this book helped him to be a better leader and teammate. Kobe single-handedly won the most important game on his way to winning the championship . . . he won the leadership game.

You, like Kobe, can become a better teammate and help your team be the best version of themselves by bringing out the best in everyone. Your performance does not mean much if your teammates struggle or the team performance suffers. That is why champion teammates become strong leaders. You can become the leader you always hoped to be.

In Part III of this book, you will be introduced to effective ways to up your game and master your leadership craft as a teammate. When we experience athlete leaders in today's cultures, many continue to rely on strategies and methodologies that are obsolete. Team captains often are chosen because they are a senior, possess the best ability, are the most vocal, or possess many other characteristics that do not necessarily exemplify leadership. None of these translate into legitimate reasons for being a team leader.

If you wish to be a successful, influential, powerful, and compelling leader, the next section will help you master a way to better serve, lead, inspire, and empower your teammates. We want to guide you to be a champion teammate by practicing certain traits, behaviors, and characteristics such as courage, compassion, commitment, patience, persistence, integrity, selflessness, vulnerability, humility, love, and modesty, to name a few.

The Chinese call this *jingshen*, a Mandarin concept meaning "to instill spirit, vitality, chi, passion, and personal power." *Jingshen* is a way to create environments which will help others to open their hearts to you and become better teammates. This shift in your leadership approach will allow you to be influential in helping to serve them. You will learn in this section how to cultivate strong character, be a samurai warrior who leads at a high level, and how to never be too big to do the little things. We will teach you how to use gratefulness as a way to give back, and how to be flexible and humble while executing these leadership strategies.

When you lead in this way, you win the hearts of your teammates and help your team take upon themselves the hardship, sacrifice, and suffering so essential to the achievement of the team's mission. Everyone will choose to give a little more of themselves than they thought was possible. And you will lead the way.

18. Grab the Hose

The most powerful leadership tool you have is your own personal example.
—John Wooden, 10-time NCAA champion
basketball coach at UCLA

Jerry is often asked the question, "How did you learn so much about being a servant leader—and when?" The answer is simple. He learned all he needed to know to lead at the ripe old age of 12. Jerry claims that he was the luckiest kid in his Brooklyn, New York, neighborhood because his father was a battalion chief in the New York City Fire Department. He would take Jerry to work once a week in the summer, and he went to fires in the back seat of the chief's car, watching his dad lead a team of firefighting warriors into raging, burning buildings, using all the traits of a champion teammate. The most powerful trait Jerry learned was to lead by example.

One blistering, hot summer afternoon in Manhattan when they arrived at a warehouse fire, there were four other officers standing outside, barking orders to the firefighters to run into the flaming building. They led by shouting commands, and it wasn't going well. Everyone carrying the hose seemed paralyzed in place, afraid the risk and danger were too great. Jerry remembers, as if it were yesterday, how his five-foot-seven dad jumped out of the chief's car, sprinted to the front, grabbed the hose, and shouted out to his men, "Follow me," as he took off into the smoky, burning building, climbing the stairs and demonstrating what had to be done. He led by example, and this influence reverberated throughout the entire scene, with other officers and firemen imitating this diminutive warrior.

Jerry remembers how proud he was of him and how everyone began to take initiative and put out the fire. Jerry subsequently learned how his dad's team was in awe of him, how much they respected him, and that they would go the distance if he asked them to do so. Many years later, after his father retired and passed away, Jerry visited the same fire station where he'd worked, and there was a photo of his father on the wall near the front door. He was considered an icon, a leader who many years later would still be influencing others by his example. Why? Because he was not afraid to Grab the Hose.

While Jerry didn't have a name for what his dad was doing at that time, he knew it was special. It was Jerry's good fortune to have this experience, as his father's leadership behaviors permeated Jerry's nervous system. These traits carried over into Jerry's adult life, first teaching English literature and coaching a team of basketball athletes, leading men as an officer in the Navy during Vietnam, and now, 50 years later, still teaching, coaching, and leading as his father did. His father was educationally limited, only going to school through the eighth grade, yet was a brilliant role model for what it takes to guide and lead others to be the best teammate they can be.

Jerry's dad never felt he was too big to do the little things. He was the hardest worker of the entire group. You are capable of being a similar type of high-impact teammate and leading by example. It is your work ethic that will have the most influence on your teammates. Begin to model for others exactly what behaviors you hope your teammates will demonstrate. How do you do this?

First, take on the unwanted work of the team, especially when no one is looking. If you want your team to be calm, passionate, focused, caring, connective, and courageous, then you must be intent on being the same way. If you want your teammates to show up on time, to work hard, and to stay late, then you must embrace these actions yourself. Don't just talk about it or point out the problems. Do the work and lead by example. In this way, your credibility and influence will expand. Mahatma Gandhi taught us this lesson: *Be the change you want to see.*

Be mindful and aware of how your actions impact everyone. Be respectful to the officials, to the other team, to the fans, and your teammates will follow suit. Talking behind the back of another, criticizing them and demeaning their efforts, will diminish your power to influence, and you will lose the respect of others. Using foul language or falling short of team standards will lessen your leadership influence throughout the entire team.

You are capable of being a leader, and it starts with leading by example. Be what you desire from your teammates. Grab the hose!

Optimize Your Performance

1. What are three specific ways for you to demonstrate leading your teammates by example?

_____

_____

_____

2. What do you need to *start* doing—that you are not currently doing—to lead by example?

_____

_____

_____

3. What do you need to *stop* doing—that you are currently doing—to lead by example?

_____

_____

_____

4. What can you do specifically to stay mindful of leading by example on a daily basis?

_____

_____

_____

5. What specifically did you learn from Chief Lynch's leadership as it applies to being an exceptional teammate?

_____

_____

_____

19. Sweep the Shed

Sweeping the sheds. Doing it properly. So no one else has to. Because no one looks after the All Blacks. The All Blacks look after themselves.

—James Kerr, author of *Legacy*

We often start many of our team workshops by asking the gathered group, "Do you know who the most successful team of the professional sports era is?" The hands go up and the usual answers come out: "Real Madrid!" "The New York Yankees!" "The Boston Celtics!" Typically, after five or six wrong answers, we eventually hear the correct one, usually not stated with much conviction.

"The New Zealand All Blacks?"

Yes, the New Zealand All Blacks, a rugby powerhouse that has won nearly 80 percent of their games over a 120-year stretch through 2021, including three World Cup titles and astonishing success that has seen only seven national teams in the world ever beat them. It is an extraordinary record of excellence, culture, and continued reinvention, cycling through different leaders, coaches, and new players, yet all with one goal in mind: leave the shirt in a better place.

In the outstanding book about the All Blacks called *Legacy*, author James Kerr discusses one of their core values that epitomizes the selfless, humble attitude that has helped drive this success. It's called "Sweep the Shed."

The goal of every All Blacks player is to contribute to the legacy by doing his part to grow the game and keep the team progressing every single day. In order to do so, the players realize that you must remain humble, and that no one is too big or too famous to do the little things required each and every day to get better. You must eat right. You must sleep well. You must take care of yourself on and off the field. You must train hard. You must sacrifice your own goals for the greater good and a higher purpose. And, you must sweep the shed.

After each match, played in front of 60,000-plus fans and millions more on TV, after the camera crews have left and the coaches are done speaking, when the eyes of the world have turned elsewhere, there is still a locker room to be cleaned. And that job belongs to the players.

After each and every game, the All Blacks leading players take turns sweeping the locker room of every last piece of grass, tape, and mud. Their captains and senior players are the first to pick up the brooms. They lead by example, and the younger players follow. No one is too big or too important to get out of cleaning the locker room, because it is a symbol of humility and never being above doing the little things, the seemingly meaningless details that aggregate over time to make the difference in a close game. As James Kerr concludes, "Sweeping the sheds. Doing it properly. So no one else has to. Because no one looks after the All Blacks. The All Blacks look after themselves."

Whenever we begin work with a new team, we always check out the locker room. Is it clean and orderly, or a disaster? Do people pick up after themselves, or do they expect someone to do it for them? Today's collegiate and professional athletes often have endless amounts of support services, from nutritionists to athletic trainers to support staff who wash their uniforms and clean up after them. It is very easy for your ego to get in the way and start to expect that you can let the small things go because someone will always be there to pick up after you. But will they be there during crunch time on the field, on the ice, on the court? No, they won't.

In the critical moments of competition, the only people who can take care of the details are you and your teammates. If you live day-to-day expecting someone else to do the dirty work, what makes you think that on game day you and your team will have it in you to do what it takes to make that one extra play, to exhibit that one additional moment of discipline? Chances are, in the biggest moments, you will not.

The greatest teams, and the best teammates, are humble and hungry. They sweep the shed. In 2021, John was entering his fourth year with the Rutgers University women's field hockey program. They had made tremendous strides as a program, consistently in the NCAA Top 15, competing in every single game, and defeating numerous ranked opponents year after year. They had done tremendous work during COVID to improve individually, and to build their family and sense of belonging. The 2021 team had the physical ability, mental fortitude, leadership, and spiritual talent to be the best team in program history. The biggest concern for John was whether seeing that, the team would start ignoring some of the small details. That concern was alleviated in August of 2021 during preseason.

After a team meal in the brand-new student athletic center, John was sitting with head coach Meredith Civico and her staff, along with the team captains and a longtime strength and conditioning coach from Rutgers. As the meal came to an end, without being asked, everyone on the team began doing their part to clean up after themselves. Some players boxed up the leftovers. Others wiped down the tables and threw out the trash. As everyone left, they tucked in their chairs. A couple of upperclassmen actually made a special box of food to go for the strength coach to bring home to his family.

As the team said their goodbyes, the strength coach turned to the coaches and said, "I have been here 25 years and I have never seen a team do that before. They usually just leave the place trashed and expect someone else to pick up after them." That's sweeping the shed. They had arrived.

Three months later, that team was 18 and 2. They were the Big Ten women's field hockey champions, and the first team at Rutgers to win a Big Ten championship. They were the number one ranked team going into the NCAA tournament. And although they eventually fell in a shootout in the NCAA quarterfinals, and did not achieve their ultimate goal of becoming national champions, they had a tremendous, fulfilling season.

The team had done everything they could to control the controllables, and left no stone unturned. They left the shirt and the program in a far better place. They raised the standard. And they did so by being humble and hungry, demonstrating that by sweeping the sheds every single day. Because no one needed to take care of Rutgers Field Hockey. They took care of themselves.

Is your team ready to take this next step, pay attention to every little detail, and rely on no one except their teammates and coaching staff to become a champion?

Optimize Your Performance

1. Reflecting upon the stories above, how do you and your team "sweep the shed?" How do you and your team leave your home locker room, your visiting locker room, your bench areas, your team bus, and your area at restaurants?

_____

_____

_____

2. How can you and your team specifically demonstrate "sweeping the shed" every single day in practice and in games during the season and in the off-season?

_____

_____

_____

3. What is the attitude of the upperclassmen, leaders, and captains toward serving their teammates and being leaders by sweeping the shed, picking up after practice and games, and not expecting others to serve them?

_____

_____

_____

20. Have a Humble Heart

Do not boast overly. Keep the jade and treasures reserved within the bosom.
A posture of a humble heart will bring blessings from all directions.
—Lao-Tzu, *Tao Te Ching*

As long as you don't have entitlement in your program, you've got a shot.
—Kirby Smart, two-time national champion
football coach at Georgia

Humility is one of the essential traits of great leadership and Tim Duncan, the NBA Hall of Famer and five-time NBA champion center with the San Antonio Spurs, is a perfect example of the humble leader. He consistently praised his teammates and coaches when people tried to heap accolades upon him. He did not engage in trash talking, instead letting his play do all the talking needed. And he was never above doing the small things.

In one famous story shortly after his retirement, Duncan was working out with a Spurs rookie who was out of shape after being out injured for two months. The workout was so intense that the rookie vomited all over the court. Immediately Duncan grabbed some towels and cleaned it all up, looked at the player and said, "Get back on the court, we have work to do." If a Hall of Famer wiping up the vomit of an NBA rookie is not the ultimate sign of humility, we don't know what is.

An exquisite example of humility could be observed during the era of iconic basketball coach Dean Smith at the University of North Carolina. It was he who influenced generations to come by implementing his concept of "pointing the finger." Whenever a Tarheel scored a basket off an assist from his teammate, he would humbly give credit to the teammate who gave the assist by pointing the finger at him as they ran back on defense. Deflecting attention toward other team members for their contribution to your success is the epitome of being a humble champion teammate.

One final example of humility is NBA Hall of Famer Bill Russell. He is considered one of the greatest teammates ever, in any sport. He won eleven NBA championships, two NCAA titles, and the 1956 Olympic Gold Medal, and always embraced a role of doing the dirty work for his teams. He played defense, rebounded, and blocked shots, redefining how his position was played. He could score points when called upon but was more than happy to serve and make his teammates look good. "The most important measure of how good a game I played," said Russell, "was how much better I made my teammates play." Russell was a samurai teammate.

The word *samurai* in Japanese means service with heart, honor, and integrity. In this sense, the samurai teammate is the ideal teammate, one who serves and leads the team with heart. Service is not about servitude or catering to all the wishes of your teammates. It's about valuing them and adding worth to their lives.

When you lead in the samurai way, you gain more power, not over your team but power to influence and help navigate change and growth. Samurai teammates embody profound compassion and wisdom in their consistent efforts to promote the growth of everyone on the team. Being a samurai teammate is about transformative action that can change the relationship between you and your teammates. That transformative action happens when you can

1. admit mistakes and be vulnerable,
2. mediate conflict in a cooperative way,
3. listen attentively,
4. acknowledge all opinions,
5. be patient and understanding,
6. be demanding out of love for the benefit of the growth of others,
7. catch teammates doing something right, and
8. perform acts of random kindness.

This is not to say that you cannot be happy and proud of your achievements. Cherish the moment, celebrate your efforts, and, at the same time, be aware that without your team, you would not be the athlete you are. When you think about it, all of your accomplishments in life have been the result of others' input and help. To brag, boast, or get involved with self-aggrandizement is a sure sign that you are insecure.

Oftentimes we are the recipient of praise and attention because of what we accomplish. To keep himself in line with the truth, Jerry tells himself that he is a mere hole in a flute where the breath of those much wiser than he is goes directly through him (the hole) to others who benefit from that wisdom. Without doubt, he is humbly aware that without these giants, he could not do his work and make a difference in the lives of others. So it is with you as well. Being an exceptional team-mate means to be aware that the power of your influence is directly related to the assists you have received from others in your life.

In sports, humility provides you with clarity, while arrogance makes your vision cloudy. Humility enhances your capabilities and relieves the stress and pressure of trying to hold up a false image, and in the end, you are often the recipient of praise and recognition *because* of your humble nature. Have you ever noticed that individuals who put themselves last seem to be regarded as first? As the old saying goes, "A mistake that makes you humble is better than an achievement that leaves you arrogant." That is ancient wisdom that is so meaningful in modern sports.

Athletics is an arena where many crave attention. Many feel a need to self-promote and prove their worth. A champion teammate steps aside and lets others experience the accolades of success. Such a teammate realizes that accomplishments are team-generated rather than the work of any one athlete. The humble teammate is well aware of the synergistic interdependence of the entire team.

History teaches all of us that being humble is more potent in achieving your goals and being successful than always trying to prove yourself. Ironically, the act of being humble IS success. Champion teammates like Steph Curry, Tom Brady, Abby Wambach, and others manage to hold on to their humble roots. And the magic ingredient of all special teammates is having a strong sense of self and feeling secure within.

Confucius claims that humility is the solid foundation of all virtues. The key to being a great teammate is to stay humble and never think for one moment that you are better than anyone else on the team. This will give you power, not over others, but the power to influence them in positive ways. Notice how all rivers flow to the ocean because the sea is lower. We are all humans, and we crave acceptance, connection, caring, and love in humble environments.

Optimize Your Performance

1. Here are a few of the ways to practice humility:

   a. Shower teammates with credit to help them display higher levels.

   b. Encourage your teammates to give you valuable input and opinions about your contribution or lack of it.

   c. Ask your teammates the question, "How can I be a better teammate for you?"

   _____

   _____

   d. Ask yourself, "What do I need to *start* doing—that I'm not currently doing—to be humble?"

   _____

   _____

e. Ask yourself, "What do I need to *stop* doing—that I am currently doing—to be more humble?"

_____

_____

f. Is the Tim Duncan story relevant to you as a leader?

_____

_____

2. Discuss the stories of the UNC men's basketball team, Bill Russell, and Tim Duncan. How can your team show this same level of humility? How can you share credit and acknowledge assists? How can your more-experienced team members show the level of respect to a young player like Tim Duncan did? How can your senior players do the dirty work like Bill Russell?

_____

_____

21. Walk the Talk

Character is what you really are; reputation is what people say you are.
—John Wooden, 10-time NCAA champion
basketball coach at UCLA

Many people talk a good game, but the best teammates don't just talk the talk. They walk the walk. Jerry was once working with an NCAA tennis athlete who struggled to maintain his integrity, believe in himself, and trust the power within to be resilient and courageous. It seemed to be an issue of character, failing from time to time to do the right thing, much to the chagrin of his teammates. He was down 5–0 in the first set and his attitude was defeatist: "I can't win this one so why bother to put energy into it . . . let's get to the next set."

This was a blatant misrepresentation of the spirit of sport and a failure to uphold his agreement to fight the fight till it was over. His teammates were upset by his approach to give up his effort to battle to the end. He was making a clear statement about his integrity and character. And, his behavior was disrespectful to the opponent by diminishing his triumph.

When you roll over and capitulate, you miss the opportunity to teach your opponent how a true champion competes when all looks bleak. By not letting up, this athlete would have demonstrated strong character traits had he forced his opponent to prove to the last point of the set that he deserves to be as good as the score indicated. Instead, he compromised his character by turning away from his true self and selling out because he feared failure. Champion teammates recognize that words themselves are not enough. You must follow through with proper actions.

Your words combined with your actions are the manifestation of your character, who you really are, as Coach Wooden states above. Character is a virtue that requires ethical strength and integrity. Champion teammates are high-character individuals. Regardless of circumstances, they are committed to upholding their personal principles and doing the right thing. This athlete did not do the right thing and failed himself. Worse, his team suffered because they lost confidence in him as they were moving into national championships.

The *Tao Te Ching*, an ancient book of leadership, talks about how doing the right thing is strength of character. Here is what this book teaches:

> *Hold to your ethics and principles*
> *Stand strongly for what you hold true.*
> *Believe in your true self and trust in*
> *the power within and use it. Act in concert*
> *with your dreams and visions.*

Only by being true to yourself can you be the champion teammate that you hope to be. And you must back up your words with actions.

If you want your team to trust you, you must be trustworthy as a teammate. But you must understand that trust is not simply about your ability. Trust is intimately connected with strong character. It is about being dependable on the good days and bad days, about walking the talk and not just talking the walk. And trust is about being a bit vulnerable and admitting when you are wrong. You gain trust by under promising and over delivering. Saying things that you don't mean sends mixed messages, which are confusing for your teammates. You gain trust by walking the walk.

When teammates see cracks in the character dam, they naturally choose to walk away from your influence, making it highly unlikely that they'll ever follow your lead. Here is a list of the top character traits that you can focus on that will help demonstrate strength of character and build trust with your teammates:

- Dependability
- Flexibility
- Gratefulness
- Honesty
- Humility
- Kindness
- Patience
- Positivity
- Selflessness

As a teammate, you are challenged with character issues every day; you need to find innovative ways to deal with those challenges. But remember that you can't run a popularity contest with your teammates either. You will always be met with some opposition if you follow your heart and stick to what you intuitively know is right. Standards matter, and the best way to uphold them is to walk the walk every single day.

Optimize Your Performance

1. How does the tennis story help you to develop strong character as a teammate?

    _____

    _____

    _____

2. Which team member demonstrates the character traits that you most admire? What specifically are these traits? What can you do today to demonstrate ONE of these traits and try the others in days to come?

    _____

    _____

    _____

3. Take the answers to the above exercise and write the behaviors or traits on small cards, as you would an affirmation, and read them to yourself each day after your mindful meditation visualization.

4. Ask your teammates which aspects of your character are helpful, and which you need to improve. They can write these out anonymously. Then look for patterns in their responses about your strong points. Are there any traits that stand out consistently? Keep what's good and work on what needs improvement. By doing this, you communicate to your team that you care about self-improvement and change, which is a strong character trait in itself.

22. Pet the Dragons

*You cannot solve a problem until you acknowledge that you
have one and accept responsibility for solving it.*
— Zig Ziglar, motivational speaker

If you think long and hard about your life, one thing you will probably realize sooner or later is that most of life's valuable lessons were taught to you in children's books. One of my kids' favorite stories growing up was *There's NO Such Thing as a Dragon* by Jack Kent. It is a simple book about a boy named Billy who wakes up one morning and finds a dragon in his room. It is a cute dragon, very small, and he pets it as it follows him downstairs for breakfast. When he tells his mom about the dragon, she smiles and replies, "There's no such thing as a dragon." All of a sudden, the dragon grows.

As Billy goes about his day, the dragon continues to grow every time it is not acknowledged. It eats his pancakes, continues to get in the way of everything, and soon fills the entire house. Yet each time Billy calls attention to the dragon, his mother tells him, "There's no such thing as a dragon." Every time she says it, the dragon grows bigger. Finally, the dragon is so big it runs off with the house, with Billy and his mom in it. When his father comes home for lunch, the house is gone, and he has to go find it. When he asks his wife how this happened, Billy yells out, "It was the dragon," and his mom starts to reply, in her familiar refrain, "There's no such thing . . ."

"But there is a dragon," says Billy, "a very big dragon," and he pets it on the head. And just as fast as the dragon grew, it started to shrink, back to the size of a kitten. "I don't mind dragons this size," says his mother. "Why did it have to grow so big?"

"I'm not sure," says Billy, "but I think it just wanted to be noticed."

The lesson of this story is a simple one: There are dragons in all of our lives, and if we acknowledge them and work to solve them, they stay small. But if we ignore them, sweep them under the rug, and hope they go away, they grow and grow until they take over our home, our family, and our lives. And yes, they can take over our team as well.

There is no team in the world that does not have dragons in the locker room. Those come with being part of a team. They may be around playing time, positions, roles and responsibilities, commitment, fitness, or a litany of other things. Your team has dragons. The difference between average teams and championship teams is what you do about them. Average teams ignore them and hope they go away. Great teams Pet the Dragon.

Leadership can be a burden, and one of the greatest burdens you will carry is having to acknowledge and pet your dragons. You may have to call out teammates, friends, even family members, for not meeting the team standards or for not buying into the culture. You may have to risk being liked and seek being respected by calling out behaviors that are letting the team down.

We have seen this with teams we work with on everything from being on time, competitiveness in training, and fitness levels to treatment of teammates, development of cliques within the team, and off-field behaviors, such as drinking and drugs, that not only hurt performance but destroy team trust and unity. True leaders are brave and not afraid to step up and pet the dragon.

John loves to introduce the story of dragons as a metaphor with his teams. When he first visited the Rutgers field hockey team in 2018, he decided to read them *There's NO Such Thing as a Dragon*, and was worried they would laugh him out of the locker room. But they did not. They understood that their team, like every other, had dragons. They had all been part of teams that failed to pet their dragons, and as a result the team suffered.

Petting the dragon became one of their commitments to each other, so John bought the team a plastic toy dragon for the locker room. To this day, the dragon sits at the front of the locker room, a constant reminder to keep their small problems small. And since that time, the team has built an incredible culture, consistently achieved Top 10 national rankings, won the Big Ten championship for the first time in program history, and achieved a number one NCAA ranking in 2021, all by keeping their dragons small.

As a leader you will be given the opportunity to pet the dragons on your team, and it takes courage to do so. If you want to be taken seriously, you must do a few things:

1. First and foremost, you must epitomize your team values. You cannot lecture your team on values if you yourself do not live up to them. If you want to talk about effort at training, then your effort must be exemplary. If you want to talk about being on time, then you better be on time.

2. You must hold everyone accountable for agreed-upon behaviors. You cannot look the other way when your friends or classmates break team standards but try to call out others. You also should not call out the whole team if just one or two people are responsible. Be specific.

3. You must remind your team that these are the team values/agreed-upon behaviors and can be changed at any time, but if we all agree to these things, then we must uphold them.

4. You must recognize that conflict is OK and is part of team building.

5. You must give space for others to be heard and help those who are breaking the team standards see their behavior through the eyes of their teammates and not just you.

Leadership is hard, but the stronger the culture you build, the more you sacrifice your personal ambitions for those of the team, and the more you exemplify and live out your values in front of the team, the more buy-in you will get from your teammates. Everyone you play has dragons in their locker room. Have the courage to pet yours!

Optimize Your Performance

1. Read *There's NO Such Thing as a Dragon* by Jack Kent as a team. Then have an honest discussion by breaking into groups and identifying the biggest dragons your team needs to acknowledge. How can you solve these problems? Write down your takeaways here.

_____

_____

_____

2. Buy a plastic or stuffed dragon and put it in your locker room or team room. Whenever there is an issue that needs acknowledging, grab the dragon and get everyone's attention. Acknowledge the issues, and come up with a solution moving forward. Some issues will come up more than once, so be prepared to revisit some issues numerous times.

3. Practice having difficult conversations through role-playing. For example, Athlete 1 needs to speak with Athlete 2 because they are not giving enough effort in practice. Help guide the conversation.

23. Give Everyone a Role

When we tell people to do their jobs, we get workers.
When we trust people to do their jobs, we get leaders.
— Simon Sinek, author of *Start with Why*

If you had asked Fordham University men's soccer coach Jim McElderry prior to the 2017 season which player on his roster might score the biggest goal of the season, his answer probably would not have been Jordan Black. Even if you had asked him that same question on the eve of their NCAA Sweet 16 matchup against Duke University, the name Jordan Black likely would not have come up. And yet, on the evening of November 25, 2017, Black scored arguably the biggest goal in school history, scoring the goal in the tenth round of a penalty kick shootout that sent the Rams to their first ever NCAA Elite Eight. Why not Black?

Before stepping up to take the game-winning kick, Black, a senior backup goalkeeper from New Jersey, had not played a single minute all season. In fact, he had only appeared in four total games his entire career. Why was a career backup who had not played a minute all season taking the biggest kick in program history? Because Black was an incredible teammate.

Jordan Black was what we might call a top 10 percenter. He was a guy who showed up early and stayed late to help his teammates. He was a glue guy, bringing positive energy and enthusiasm to games and training. He was a great student and an example in the classroom. He was the type of guy that, according to McElderry, you could never leave off a travel roster even if you knew he wouldn't play. "The guys just loved Jordan. He inspired everyone around him to be better." That is why Jordan Black stood over the biggest kick in Fordham men's soccer history on November 25, 2017, and etched his name forever in the record books. Jordan Black was an incredible teammate. Jordan Black was given a role and a way to contribute to his team even without playing a minute.

When we begin working with new programs, we pay as much attention to what is happening on the sidelines as we do to what is happening on the field. The attitude, focus, and engagement of those players who are not getting in the game often tells us much more about the culture of the program than the performance on the field. Are they standing or sitting? Are they cheering or chatting with a teammate about an unrelated subject? Are they celebrating our goals and successful plays, or has their attention wandered? We cannot stress enough how important it is for everyone to be all in, and how impactful a sideline or bench full of engaged teammates can be on performance.

In our experience everyone is usually dialed in during preseason. But as soon as we start playing games and a depth chart or playing hierarchy starts to emerge, it can be very easy for teammates to tune out. They do not see themselves as important, since they are not playing many minutes during the game. The coaches start focusing on the players who will play in the next game, and pay less attention to those who might not. These teammates' effort and focus often drops at practice, and soon they are going through the motions, not pushing the players ahead of them in the depth chart, and falling further behind. It is up to you as a leader to make sure everyone knows they have a role and that they matter and can contribute even without playing a minute.

John once had a conversation with an NCAA athlete who was frustrated with her playing time. She was stuck behind an All-American midfielder and barely seeing the field. He had to convince her of two things. First, her teammate was an All-American because of how hard she was pushing her in practice. And second, what an opportunity she had to improve. She got to go one-on-one every day in training with the best player at her position in the country. No one else had such an opportunity to learn, so take advantage of it.

The importance of giving everyone a role became especially clear during the pandemic that began in 2020, when all of a sudden illness could knock out multiple players in the depth chart very quickly. Some of our teams played important league and playoff games with players who had not yet played a minute that season because of a last-minute COVID outbreak. The teams that kept everyone fit and connected were able to overcome these moments, and go into games feeling confident, knowing that their teammates were ready to step in.

Great leaders pay attention to everyone in the group and use their influence to elevate their teammates (remember the RIVER). They make time to reach out and connect, catch them being good, and invest in their development. Steve Kerr once told us that although he won five NBA championships as a player, he was usually a reserve on all those teams. As a result, he pays a lot of attention to the reserves on his bench, keeps them on their toes and ready to go, and makes the time to learn how he can coach them better. You must do the same, because you never know if you will need them with the game on the line. Just ask Jordan Black.

Optimize Your Performance

1. Here are some things you can do to help everyone on your team feel that they are valued:

    a. Reward your values: You don't have to be a starter or top athlete to be gritty, have a positive attitude, or be the hardest worker. Most team values are things that are attainable by every team member, so pay attention to those whose accolades might not come on game day and recognize their contribution.

    b. Point to the bench after a big basket or a goal, or run over and celebrate with them on the sideline if appropriate. Make team success inclusive.

    c. Come early or stay after with a reserve teammate and help them improve their game. Be a teacher and mentor, especially if they are younger than you. And in practice, catch them being good.

2. Gather with your teammates and answer the following questions:

    a. What do we need to *start* doing—that we are not currently doing—to make everyone on the team feel like they have a role?

    _____

    _____

b. What do we need to *stop* doing—that we are currently doing—that is excluding some teammates and making them believe they are not contributing to the team?

_____

_____

_____

c. What do we need to *keep* doing—that we are currently doing—that is building our team camaraderie and making everyone feel that they matter?

_____

_____

_____

24. Learn to Surf

What you're supposed to do when you don't like a thing is change it. If you can't change it, change the way you think about it. Don't complain.
—Maya Angelou, poet, author

You can't stop the waves, but you can learn to surf.
—Jon Kabat-Zinn, Zen teacher and author

By the time the 2015 FIFA Women's World Cup rolled around, US women's national team soccer player Abby Wambach had achieved nearly everything in her stellar career. She had been FIFA World Player of the Year. She had won two Olympic gold medals, played in five World Cups and three Olympics, and scored more international goals than any woman in the history of the game. Yet in 2015, she was 35 years old, her skills were diminishing, and she found herself benched during her final chance to win the one prize that had eluded her—the World Cup.

When Coach Jill Ellis pulled Wambach aside during the tournament and told her she would no longer be starting, she was devastated. For 24 hours she stewed, she cried, and her emotions nearly got the best of her. But then she had an epiphany. She realized that her legacy would be defined by her behavior and attitude at that moment.

Instead of whining, complaining, or becoming a disruption to the team, Wambach decided to not only accept but embrace her new role. "I had a choice to decide what kind of teammate I was. What kind of a person I was," said Wambach in an interview afterward. "It was the greatest test of my life, and it is one of the most difficult things that I had to go through. And I do know that looking back from my death-bed, it is one of the things that I am most proud of, because I instilled and held up my values and integrity through this, which was one of the hardest things in my life. It taught me everything I needed to know about leadership."

Wambach went from starting player to emotional and spiritual leader on the bench. She cheered on her teammates. She helped support and mentor the younger players. When she was subbed on, she hustled and did the dirty work, making a difference and helping close out games. And after beating Japan 5–2 in the final, she finally got to lift the World Cup trophy. But she got so much more than that. "If you're not a leader on the bench," wrote Wambach, "don't call yourself a leader on the field. You're either a leader everywhere or nowhere."

Abby Wambach, perhaps the greatest women's soccer player of all time, taught us all a huge lesson in 2015. When things with your team are not going how you'd like them to, there's a tendency to whine and complain, creating unnecessary drama for everyone. It is very common for us to desire life as we want it to be rather than as it is. Yet this causes us to suffer. The unpleasant behavior that happens when conditions are not just the way you would like them often makes you a very undesirable teammate. It gets you nowhere. In fact, you are distracting yourself and others from the tasks at hand, resulting in lackluster performances for all.

If you can't seem to cope with how things are, follow the advice of Jon Kabat-Zinn who says, "If you can't stop the waves, learn how to surf." Do this by changing how you see things. You end your suffering and move forward when you accept things as they are, just like Abby Wambach did. The waves did not stop for Wambach. In fact, in the defining moment of her career, with the world watching, the waves were huge. She just learned to surf.

Anson Dorrance, head women's soccer coach at the 22-time national champion University of North Carolina, mentions how he, his staff, and the team have zero tolerance for distractions that take the focus off the good of the team. In fact, they explicitly have "No whining, no drama, no complaining" as one of their core values. Being a good teammate is defined as holding others accountable for this team rule. Complaining, to them, is a strong indication that the whiner is out of control. Their mission is to have that person self-regulate or step aside. They all strive to be good teammates in this regard.

Complaining happens on many teams, but think how destructive it is. It doesn't solve any problems and actually takes away the time and energy to improve your environment. No one wants to hear you complain either. Of course not. Your life, and your team, starts to improve the moment you stop complaining!

The cure for such behaviors is to practice positivity and focus on getting better and giving to others, as opposed to complaining about not getting what you think you deserve. All your complaints, drama, whining, and excuses never bring you anything but more grief. They never bring you closer to your dreams. If you think you deserve more, ask yourself, what must I do to earn it? Then you will be acting like an exceptional teammate.

There will always be times when life does not go our way. Life will at times seem unfair. That is life. But vocalizing it and complaining about it will keep you stuck as you lose the respect and trust of your teammates. Even if you can justify your complaining, by continuing to whine about how unfair things are, it keeps you incarcerated in your mind, preventing you from exploring how to go forward and be the best teammate you can be, as well as the best athlete you could possibly be. To paraphrase Bob Marley, emancipate yourself from such inner slavery. Your mind can liberate you if you so choose.

Optimize Your Performance

1. Discuss the story about Abby Wambach as a group. How did her choice to become a champion teammate instead of a distraction cement her legacy and help her team win a World Cup? How can you help our teammates if you see them going down the rabbit hole of complaining and vocalizing negative thoughts about their role, coaches, other teammates, etc.?

   _____

   _____

2. To bypass this rut and dig yourself out of this rabbit hole and become a champion teammate, how can you (a) stay positive, (b) work hard, (c) control your perceptions and thoughts, and (d)) make a strong effort not to vocalize your negative thoughts?

   _____

   _____

   _____

3. Here is a provocative tale that teaches how to learn to surf when you can't stop the waves. In what ways can this tale help you to not whine or complain when things don't go your way?

   Somewhere in ancient India, there was a king whose feet were very sensitive. He complained constantly about the kingdom's roads being rough and rocky. Finally, he decided to have all the roads paved with leather so his feet would be comfortable. He asked the best craftsmen in the land to bid on this enormous project. One responded that he could do the job, but it would cost enormous sums of money. Then, a woman came to the king and said I can do it for 10 rupees, a very small sum. Her approach was to strap a piece of leather under each of his feet, and, in this way, he would be walking on leather wherever he went. When the complaining stopped, a solution was discovered.

25. Choose Joy

*One of the reasons they are so special is that they have joy in the process of
each practice and game, day after day. It is an integral part of our success.
It comes from enjoying everything every day.*

—Steve Kerr, head coach, Golden State Warriors

*The warrior's approach is to say "yes" to life: "yes" to it all.
We cannot cure the world of sorrows, but we can choose to live in joy.*

—Joseph Campbell

One of the foundational pieces of being an exceptional teammate is
your ability to generate joy in your environment. Much of this book
emphasizes the why, how, and what of service because service is joy. We
are all about embracing the concept of "servant leadership" as a healthy,
joyful way to lead. In a recent conversation that Jerry had with Golden
State Warriors Coach Steve Kerr, he mentioned how his number one
core value for the team is joy, and much of that joy is created by the
vibe of service with the guys, an environment of giving rather than
getting.

One of the activities he mentioned that demonstrates service is
how they all share dinner together often. Perhaps on a holiday, they all
congregate at Steph Curry's home to be served dinner, be with family,
and laugh with the kids and spouses. While on the road, they will eat

together often. At the practice facility, there is music, singing, laughter, and an abundance of playfulness. What Steve told Jerry is that in their culture, joy is the reward. It is an in-the-moment concept. There is no path to joy; joy is the path.

We have worked with hundreds of champion cultures and athletes. What we observe is how often these cultures seem to be joyful and happy. Are they happy because they are champions, or are they champions because they are happy? We believe that both matter but the latter is the biggest factor in the making of a champion. From this we suggest that you are a more exceptional teammate when you are joyful. As Norman Vincent Peale suggests, "Think joy, talk joy, practice joy, share joy, saturate your mind with joy, and you will have the time of your life today and every day all of your life."

Joy, like happiness, is a habit that can be developed through your daily thoughts, which then impact actions. It's a choice. Steph Curry is a very joyful teammate who practices positive thinking, and he influences his teammates by demonstrating elevated emotions such as joy. But we all need to remember that a big part of joy involves the thrill of hard work and even some suffering. The suffering enables you to appreciate the joyful moment, like needing darkness to fully appreciate the light. Embracing harsh and challenging times helps you to reach higher levels of joy.

Being a champion teammate means bringing the gift of joy to your team. Joyful people stay connected to others, and this carries over to performance for everyone. That's what good teammates are all about. They intuitively know that you may not always perform your best when joyful, but to perform well, you must have joy. And truth be known, all of us crave joy. Do you want to play for a joyless coach? Do you want to have unhappy and uninspiring teammates to compete with? If you meet a partner for life, do you hope there is no joy in your relationship? Of course not. After decades of working with coaches and athletes, we have never found any one person who doesn't crave joy in their environment. Joy is right up at the top of the list when asked what they want most from those with whom they spend most of their time.

Joy is healthy for all of us at all times. Medical science has proven that such exuberance impacts illness in a positive way. It relieves depression, anxiety, and stress, all elements that hinder performance. In the words of Brené Brown, "A joyful life is not a floodlight of joy. A joyful life is made up of joyful moments gracefully strung together by trust, gratitude, inspiration, and faith." So don't overthink it. Look for those small moments of joy and happiness, and string together as many of them as possible.

Optimize Your Performance

1. How does the story of the Golden State Warriors inspire you to find ways to celebrate and bring joy to your team? Can you do more team dinners, hikes, or community service to bring your group closer together?

2. In all of the championship cultures we have influenced, we make a point of encouraging all the teammates to commit to letting go of the following emotional vampires, or habits that block the path to joy. We now invite you to give up the following obstacles to becoming a champion teammate. If everyone on the team adheres to this request, joy will proliferate. Even if all don't buy in, the joy factor will improve exponentially, and if nothing else, you will be more joyful and happier. On teams with an abundance of joy, people are willing to give up the following:

   • Always having to be right
   • Trying to control everything
   • Blaming and pointing fingers at others
   • Negative self-talk
   • Complaining or whining when life doesn't go your way
   • Expectations of others
   • Excuses
   • Limiting beliefs
   • Fear
   • Resisting change

These top 10 obstacles to joy, when given up, impact all that you do each day in a positive way. Imagine for a moment how your life would be, how your teammates would feel, how they would perform, if you were committed to giving up these 10 elements and were the best teammate as a result. It IS a choice. Make it a conversation that you and your teammates have. Make promises to give these up and keep each other accountable and responsible. Make posters and signs about each of these and display them throughout the athletic environment. These actions will liberate your mind and free you up to be your best.

26. Go from Grateful to Great

Acknowledging the good that you already have in your life
is the foundation for all abundance.
—Eckhart Tolle, author of *A New Earth*

Looking back on his childhood, Jerry is appalled by the memory of how ungrateful he was for all he was given. He remembers one Christmas when he asked his parents if they could get him a special bike, a shiny black Schwinn cruiser with a comfy leather saddle. It was the top of the line, one which all his rich friends had, and he wanted to fit in. When his dad unveiled the bike on Christmas Day, it was not the one Jerry wanted. The family didn't have a lot of money at the time, so they opted for the lesser choice.

Jerry was devastated and his parents knew it. How insensitive they were to not get him his first choice. When he tells this story, he is still embarrassed, after all these years, for how ungrateful he was as a kid. It was he who was insensitive, and to this day, gratitude is a virtue that he holds close to his heart. Jerry makes sure that he gives back to life, each day, all that he has been given.

There is an ancient story of gratitude that parallels his. There was a poor man who walked miles to pray every day, complaining that he had no shoes, while all others around him did. It brought him to tears. Then one day, as he was crying because he had no shoes, he met a man who had no feet. This gave him a new perspective. What do you complain about? What is it that prevents you from being grateful? How can you get a different perspective?

Once while working with a freshman scholarship athlete enrolled at a major university, Jerry couldn't help but be a bit disappointed about her litany of complaints. They included not getting enough playing minutes, not getting a starting role, not getting enough scholarship money, and not getting the recognition she felt she deserved. As Jerry sat there with this athlete, he knew she was asking the wrong questions. Rather than ask, "What can I get?" she could have asked, "What have I been given?" And, he hoped, this would lead to the ultimate question, "How can I give?"

Acknowledging what you have is the first step in the gratefulness equation. Gratitude is the portal that creates significant changes in attitude from getting to giving. When we reflect on our blessings and not on our misfortunes, we create abundance, have greater overall health, and take our performance up several notches. How ironic . . . give then get. When you start focusing on the things you have been given in life, don't be surprised if your life and your attitude improves dramatically.

After 45 years in the business of sports leadership and optimal performance, Jerry's biggest takeaway is how hundreds upon hundreds of championship teams, athletes, and coaches demonstrated a commitment to being grateful for what they had as opposed to what they lacked. Why is it that all of the truly great teammates we have had the honor of meeting are filled with gratitude and humility? There seems to be a strong positive correlation between gratefulness and greatness.

It warms our hearts when we experience teammates who are grateful for simply being on a team with great friends, good leaders, an opportunity to be part of something that matters, community, joy, growth, and fun, regardless of minutes, money, or the role they play. Let's be honest with ourselves. As athletes wanting to be champion teammates, we are so blessed working at something we love to do.

Being aware of this begins deep within our hearts, and that is our source of gratitude.

There are so many benefits to be accrued by being grateful. It reduces negativity, rewires your brain to a more elevated set of emotions, lessens stress, improves self-esteem, develops mental toughness, and raises levels of performance. It changes fear into faith and faith into courage. It brings about elevated emotions of love, compassion, and connection, the "holy trinity" of being a mindful champion teammate. It is life changing, and so we ask why anyone would not want to practice gratefulness.

Jerry has been teaching the value of gratitude in his championship cultures for decades, and John continues that work with his teams to this day. We believe that is what separates our Way of Champions, Win the Day cultures from others. Chances are when your team arrives for practice or at the competitive arena, your minds are full and your hearts empty. There is distraction caused by trivial, unimportant nonsense or heavy, weighty issues that detract from the present moment. It's one thing to be aware and mindful of the important role gratitude plays in being an extraordinary teammate, but it is quite another to be able to implement such a virtue on a consistent basis.

The poignant words of former US President John F. Kennedy address this idea from awareness to action when he said, "As we express our gratitude, we must never forget that the highest appreciation is not to utter words, but to live them." Our teams and coaches love our work on gratefulness because it brings them back to the task of being mindfully present in the moment, mindful of why we do what we do. Therefore, try and implement the following gratefulness exercises and watch the "joy factor" rise exponentially.

Optimize Your Performance

1. How can you *start* demonstrating more gratitude to your teammates, friends, and family and focusing on all you have been given?

_____

_____

_____

2. How can you *stop* focusing on the things that you do not have at this moment so that you can bring an attitude of gratitude to your team?

_____

_____

_____

3. With your team, share a story about a time in your life when you failed to focus on gratitude. How about a story about a time with your team? What specifically can you do to demonstrate more gratitude as an exceptional teammate?

    _____

    _____

    _____

4. Before you begin your workout, training session, or work for the day, ask all team members, coaches included, to think of seven aspects of life that make them feel gratitude. For example: their skills, talents, minds, health, family, friends, opportunities, and work. Now, with eyes closed, we ask that you connect to the feeling of being grateful. Give yourself a minute to get this feeling. Then say, "Imagine this feeling coming into your body in three deep breaths, as each breath surrounds the heart. Hold each breath there as the feeling begins to expand." With this sensation of gratitude in the heart, ask yourself to make your performance as an athlete AND teammate today a reflection and extension of being grateful. Open your eyes and take on the day's tasks. Feel your vitality and positive attitude about bringing your best, and be the best teammate you can be.

5. Another gratitude exercise we use in our coaching is to have our teams sit in a circle and ask them to tell the teammate to their left why they are grateful for them as a person and as a significant athlete on the team. The room becomes inundated with love as the bond between teammates gets even stronger. This works especially well prior to a big tournament or at other significant times during the season.

6. Write a daily message of gratitude via text, email, or however you communicate to a teammate, friend, or family member and set a positive tone for your day. Begin your message with "I know I don't say this enough but . . ." When you give love, you get it back a hundred times. When we do this, we feel more optimistic, more alive, and better about life. It has been scientifically shown that such gratitude increases the activity in the brain's pleasure centers.

27. Go Slower, Arrive Sooner

Patience is a form of wisdom. It demonstrates that we understand and accept the fact that sometimes things must unfold in their own time.

—Jon Kabat-Zinn, Zen teacher and author

There was once an Olympic-caliber runner who was determined to make the US Olympic team in the 1,500-meter race. She went to her coach and asked, "How long would it be before I could make the team?" He responded, "It will take eight years."

Upset that she would have to wait that long, she said to him, "What if I increase my training, work harder, and do all the right things. How long would it take then?" He quickly responded, "In that case, you will probably get injured or burned out and have to take so much time off it will probably take twelve years."

You see, when you are in such a hurry to get results, you rarely achieve them. Impatience comes with collateral damage such as injury and burnout. When you force things to happen on a specific timetable, it causes stress and tension and things will backfire. The secret is to go slower, arrive sooner.

As you embark on your journey of being a champion teammate, know that it can't be rushed. It takes time and patience with all of its setbacks as you try to forge ahead. It is a slow, gradual, incremental process that unfolds at the right moment. This gradual process in Japanese is called *kaizen*. It was the essential ingredient and element of Japan's enormous success when rebuilding their culture from the complete devastation suffered during World War II.

Kaizen happens in a safe, cooperative, connected, caring environment where everyone does their share while fulfilling their role in the process. This concept is recognized worldwide as a necessary part of growing a strong, successful culture in business and, now, in athletics. Whether becoming an extraordinary coach, athlete, or teammate, your process of developing excellence will require you to adopt the concept of *kaizen*.

For starters, we ask you to trust the *kaizen* process. No rushing allowed. Take the time to inhale and digest all that this book will teach you. If you read it correctly, you will first scan the contents and then go back and choose those parts that leap off the page and hit you between the eyes. The journey to be a champion teammate is like a river. It has many reversals, setbacks, plateaus, and advances. There are many sprints and delays as well as times of slowing down. All this is a natural progression of how to live a great life. There are no quick fixes.

All extraordinary leaders and teammates trust, accept, and understand this process. When you grow daisies, you would never think of pulling them up in order to accelerate their growth. Being an exceptional teammate is no different. No panic needed; no fear allowed. After over 50 years of coaching and becoming more mindful, Jerry is always proud to say he is only halfway there. Jerry still experiences the failures and setbacks as well as the strides and gains. He navigates it well because he is not trying to get anywhere. He simply goes slower and arrives sooner as he works at enjoying this slow *kaizen* process.

Understand the value of having no destination. The joy is in the execution of the plan to be your best as you master your craft and make a difference. Waiting to grow and expand your skill set may be tough to take, but the fruit it bears is sweet. The important thing to remember is not how difficult the wait is but to keep a good attitude while waiting. Rapid growth and advancement are unnatural. Avoid haste and enjoy the moment of coming into your own.

It's important that you don't think of patience as the capacity to endure. Instead, see it as an opportunity to be at peace as you take the time to work at being better at what you do, regardless of how long it takes. According to nature's laws there is a natural flow to all things—chaos results when you try to hasten the natural process.

Think for a moment about the race between the tortoise and the hare. Through consistent, gradual, deliberate, steady, and slow movement, the tortoise, albeit naturally slower, arrives sooner than the quicker hare. Let that be your athletic journey as well.

We want you to remember that being a valuable teammate requires you to be a lifelong learner. That's why you continue to read books like this. You seek wisdom, as do we. The quest itself is the reward. It feels incredible to simply search and find more meaning in life. That is what you do when you patiently slow down and become the ideal teammate.

As you traverse the metaphorical desert in search of your destination, refuse to call a halt to the slow journey and trust that the palm trees will finally begin to appear on the horizon. Patience and perseverance are essential traits for you to develop as you become the best teammate you can be. Stay the course and never give up.

We quote here from a 2,500-year-old tome on leadership, the *Tao Te Ching*:

Hold to the inner vision of gradual flowering of your potential.
Avoid haste and enjoy the moment of waiting to be.

Optimize Your Performance

1. What are the top three ways that can help you to demonstrate patience?

   _____

   _____

2. How can you adapt the phrase "Go Slower, Arrive Sooner" as it relates to your journey as a great teammate or higher-level athlete?

   _____

   _____

3. What are three things that make you impatient, and what specifically can you do to change these to help you be more effective?

   _____

   _____

4. What can you *start* doing—that you're not currently doing—to be a more patient teammate?

5. What can you *stop* doing—that you are currently doing—to be a more patient teammate?

6. How can you best communicate to your teammates the value of not forcing or pushing or rushing their progress as athletes and leaders?

7. In what aspects of your life would it be helpful to apply the concept of *kaizen*? And how would that happen specifically?

_____

_____

_____

8. With your team, discuss specific ways the story about the Olympic runner influences your ability to develop your patience. What do we need to do as a team to embrace *kaizen*?

_____

_____

_____

CONCLUSION

Be Unbreakable

If you want to go fast, go alone. If you want to go far, go together.
—African Proverb

We certainly hope that you and your team have enjoyed this book and found many of its stories, activities, and lessons useful. Please keep it in your locker, in your backpack, or by your bedside, someplace you can refer to it time and again when things are not going quite as planned. As you know, things will go sideways once in a while. Life is always evolving. The only certainties are change and impermanence.

Having journeyed through this entire book, you now have a powerful tool kit that will prepare you for every team you encounter in sports and life. You have tools, strategies, lessons, and exercises to help you love and build relationships. You have principles to help you lead and engage your followers. And you have the concepts that will allow you to create a competitive cauldron that helps you and your team improve every single day. You have everything needed to have your best sports experiences and seasons ever.

There will be obstacles in your path no matter how well you plan, and no matter what you do. As the old Haitian proverb says, "Beyond mountains, there are mountains." As soon as you solve one problem, another will arise. It does not get easier as you progress in sports, school, and life. These are the terms and conditions you signed up for, and this team and others like it will help you build the capacity to endure hard things. There is joy in the execution of all the special challenges that come your way. As long as you accept them, stand up, and put one foot in front of another, you will keep moving forward in unique ways. You will keep writing your own story instead of letting others write it for you. That is the way of the champion and the exceptional teammate.

Winston Churchill, the legendary leader of Great Britain during World War II, has a quote that we often share with the teams we work with:

> To each there comes in their lifetime a special moment when they are figuratively tapped on the shoulder and offered the chance to do a very special thing, unique to them and fitted to their talents. What a tragedy if that moment finds them unprepared or unqualified for that which could have been their finest hour.

As you carefully contemplate this book, we hope you have taken the time to reflect at the end of each chapter, individually or as part of a team. Consider now how you will be better prepared when those challenging moments arise. Notice how you are now better prepared to face any obstacle, to overcome any difficulty, and turn threats, failures, and setbacks into opportunities for growth.

No matter how much you do on your own, though, you will never go as far as you will if you can build a group of like-minded teammates with a shared purpose, laughing and loving your way to victory. As the African proverb above so clearly states, you will go much further together.

In this conclusion, we have one more story to leave with you, once again from the sixth-century storyteller Aesop. An old man had a set of sons who were always fighting with one another. As he neared death, he summoned his sons to give them some parting advice and ordered his servants to bring in a bundle of sticks wrapped together. He commanded his eldest son to break it. The son strained with every muscle, but with all his efforts he was unable to break the bundle. He asked the same of each son, but none of them were successful. Next, the old man untied the bundle and handed each son a stick. "Now break them," he requested, and each son was able to easily break his stick. "You see my meaning," said their father. "Individually, you can easily be conquered, but together, one mind, one soul, you are as this bundle. You are unbreakable."

Many championship teams have used this analogy. For example, when the Golden State Warriors won the NBA championship in 2015, their mantra was "Strength in Numbers." Their team had strength, and through your union with your teammates, you have strength. This holds true for the old man's sons, and for you and your team. Never forget that.

We intend for this book to not be an ending but a beginning to encourage, inspire, and empower you to go beyond what we have to offer here and stay open to possibilities. We want to help you create a broader perspective on what it means to be a champion teammate by implementing the concepts, strategies, and tools supplied within. In this way, our book becomes a lifelong companion for stimulating wisdom, growth, and truth.

In life, there are many paths offered to the same light, and this book is just one of them.

Although the book has concluded, you haven't. There are many miles to go on your journey. There is much joy awaiting you because you will be more effective and aware of all the nuances needed to make you the impactful, exceptional teammate you hope to be.

We are very grateful for your choosing us to be part of this journey, and for your willingness to open your heart to the universal ideas in this book, both new and old. We send you much love, hope, and energy for the next step as you apply what you have learned from this book and use it to connect deeply with your teammates, lead them with a servant's heart, compete with your hair on fire, and leave the shirt in a better place. When you do, we know you will find great fulfillment and joy in these beautiful and extraordinary journeys called sports and life. The journey is about to begin. We've done our work, now it's time for you to do yours. As Joseph Campbell reminds us, "Say 'yes' to life: 'yes' to it all." Good luck!

Bibliography

Aesop. "The Father, His Sons, and the Bundle of Sticks." *Fables of Aesop*. Accessed April 11, 2023. https://fablesofaesop.com/the-father-his-sons-and-the-bundle-of-sticks.html.

Anonymous. *I Ching (Book of Changes)*. Translated by Cary F. Baynes and Richard Wilhelm. Princeton: Princeton University Press, 1997.

Branch, John. "The Haunting of Lindsey Jacobellis." *New York Times*, February 14, 2018.

Branch, John. "Long Known for a Blunder, Jacobellis Rewrites Her Story in Gold." *New York Times*, February 10, 2022.

Brown, Brené. *The Gifts of Imperfection*. Center City, MN: Hazelden Publishing, 2010.

Business Week. "Joe Torre on Winning." *Bloomberg*, August 21, 2006. https://www.bloomberg.com/news/articles/2006-08-20/joe-torre-on-winning#xj4y7vzkg.

Clear, James. *Atomic Habits: An Easy & Proven Way to Build Good Habits & Break Bad Ones*. New York: Avery, 2018.

Dorrance, Anson, and Gloria Averbuch. *The Vision of a Champion*. Chelsea, MI: Sleeping Bear Press, 2002.

Duhigg, Charles. "What Google Learned from Its Quest to Build the Perfect Team." *New York Times*, February 25, 2016.

Frankl, Viktor E. *Man's Search for Meaning*. Boston: Beacon Press, 2006.

Jackson, Phil and Hugh Delehanty. *Sacred Hoops: Spiritual Lessons of a Hardwood Warrior*. New York: Hachette, 1995.

Kent, Jack. *There's NO Such Thing as a Dragon*. New York: Random House, 1976.

Kerr, James. *Legacy: What the All Blacks Can Teach Us About the Business of Life*. London: Little, Brown Book, 2013.

Kight, Tim. "The R Factor." *Focus 3*, Accessed April 11, 2023. https://focus3.com/the-r-factor/.

Lynch, Jerry. *The Way of the Champion: Lessons from Sun Tzu's the* Art of War *and Other Tao Wisdom for Sports & Life*. Tokyo: Tuttle Publishing, 2006.

Mattingly, Don. "Being A Great Teammate." *Coachfore.org*, April 13, 2012. https://coachfore.org/2012/04/13/being-a-great-teammate-by-don-mattingly/.

Murphy, Michael. *Golf in the Kingdom*. New York: Penguin Books, 1997.

Nichiren Buddhism Library. "Many in Body, One in Mind." Accessed April 1, 2023. https://www.nichirenlibrary.org/en/dic/Content/M/63#.

Oliver, Jonah. "#272: Jonah Oliver, Performance Psychologist, on Taking Positive Action, Building Capacity to Embrace Pressure, and Finding Your Why in Order to Perform Your Best." Interview by John O'Sullivan, *Changing the Game Project*. Podcast audio. May 13, 2022. https://changingthegameproject.com/272-jonah-oliver-performance-psychologist-on-taking-positive-action-building-capacity-to-embrace-pressure-and-finding-your-why-in-order-to-perform-your-best/.

Pulisic, Christian. *Pulisic: My Journey So Far.* In collaboration with Daniel Melamud. New York: Rizzoli, 2022.

Scott, Keith. "One day a teammate or coach will have a choice to recommend you, hire you or not to hire you. . . ." Twitter, June 18, 2022, https://mobile.twitter.com/Keith_Scott05/status/1538118828525244416.

Spears, Marc J. "For Bryant, It's All About the Chase." *Yahoo!sports,* October 18, 2010. https://sports.yahoo.com/news/bryant-chase-074300609--nba.html.

Starsia, Dom. "Dear Returning College Players, It's About Today." *Inside Lacrosse,* June 1, 2018.

Tzu, Lao. *Tao Te Ching.* New York: Vintage Books, 1972.

Tzu, Sun. *The Art of War.* Chichester, England: Capstone Publishing, 2010.

Wambach, Abby. *Wolfpack: How to Come Together, Unleash Our Power, and Change the Game.* New York: Celadon Books, 2019.

Willink, Jocko. "The Scariest Navy SEAL Imaginable . . . and What He Taught Me (#107)." Interview by Tim Ferriss, *The Tim Ferriss Show.* Podcast audio. September 25, 2015. https://tim.blog/2015/09/25/jocko-willink/

Zigarelli, Michael. *The Messiah Method: The Seven Disciplines of the Winningest College Soccer Program in America.* Maitland, FL: Xulon Press, 2011.

About the Authors

Jerry Lynch and John O'Sullivan are leadership, performance, and team culture specialists. Their work has received global acclaim in youth, high school, collegiate, and professional athletics. They are highly sought after by teams, schools, and sport governing bodies around the world for their work in athletic performance, coach education, and parent engagement. Jerry and John cohost the *Way of Champions Podcast*, as well as the Way of Champions Transformational Leadership Conference, and both are national advisory board members of the Positive Coaching Alliance.

Jerry Lynch, PhD, is the founder and director of Way of Champions, a human potential and performance consulting group helping others master the relationship and culture building games in athletics, business, and life. He first learned about extraordinary performance and excellence as a nationally ranked competitive athlete sponsored by Nike, running world class times from 5,000 meters to the marathon, setting an American record in the half-marathon, and winning a national championship. He is recognized as one of the top leaders in his profession in the world. He has published 17 books in over 10 languages. Jerry has had significant influence with Olympic sports programs from New Zealand, Germany, the Philippines, and the United States. His work has impacted teams, coaches, and athletes in the NBA, Pro Lacrosse, and Major League Soccer, in addition to men's and women's basketball, lacrosse, field hockey, swimming, soccer, tennis, golf, and track and field at the universities of North Carolina, Duke, Maryland, California, Syracuse, Stanford, Harvard, and Middlebury. In the past 35 years alone, he has helped influence 118 world, national, conference and state championship teams. He has had extensive media interview coverage with CBS, NBC, and PBS national television, the *New York Times*, *Oprah Magazine*, *Sports Illustrated*, *Baltimore Sun*, *Outside Magazine* and over 400 national magazines, radio broadcasts, podcasts, and webinars. Learn more at www.WayOfChampions.com.

John O'Sullivan is the founder of Changing the Game Project, an organization dedicated to helping coaches, parents, schools, and youth sport organizations give sports back to our kids and put a little more "play" in "play ball." He is a former collegiate and professional soccer player, and has coached for over 30 years on the youth, high school, and collegiate levels. John has written two bestselling books, *Changing the Game* and *Every Moment Matters*, and his work has appeared on CNN, *Outside Magazine*, the *Huffington Post*, *Boston Globe*, ESPN, NBC Sports, and numerous other media outlets. He has consulted with the USOC, US Soccer, USA Swimming, US Ski and Snowboard, USA Wrestling, Ireland Rugby, National Rugby League of Australia, the PGA, and many other entities, including teams and coaches at Ohio State, Rutgers, Fordham, Colby, and USF. You can learn more at www.ChangingTheGameProject.com.

For bulk orders of *The Champion Teammate* please email John@ChangingTheGameProject.com